Please read and pass on.
Eventually, if you ...

Two
Paths
to
Heaven's
Gate

by Nan Dieter Conklin

Published by the National Radio Astronomy Observatory

Copyright © 2006

ISBN 0-9700411-1-X

The National Radio Astronomy Observatory is a facility of the
National Science Foundation operated
under cooperative agreement by
Associated Universities, Inc.

Associated Universities, Inc.

"For Garret, always"

Like to the lark at break of day arising

From sullen earth sings hymns at Heaven's Gate

Sonnet XXIX
W. Shakespeare

ACKNOWLEDGEMENTS

Without the enthusiastic interest of the late Sylvia Tacker and her Creative Writing Group I would never have written this story. As for publishing it, I suspect my experience is unique, because I have both enjoyed it and made new friends in the process. Claire Hooker's editing has transformed the reminiscences of an old lady into a readable story. Ellen Bouton and Patricia Smiley have shepherded the manuscript as if it were their own, and Miller Goss has made it all possible. To say thank you is not enough.

Nan Dieter Conklin
Woodinville, WA
March 2006

TABLE OF CONTENTS

FOREWARD BY MORTON S. ROBERTS

Nan was of kindergarten age when radio radiation originating from beyond the Earth's environment was first observed; a discovery that marks the birth of radio astronomy. Until then our view of the Universe, though rich and exciting, was through a tiny window—through only a small part of the electromagnetic spectrum.

Radio astronomy developed slowly, aided by physicists, electronic engineers and astronomers. A special boost to this development occurred during World War II with the massive effort devoted to microwave technology, especially that directed to radar. Interestingly, these radars inadvertently detected solar burst radiation, the subject of Nan's first published paper in 1952. This wartime event was first thought to be enemy jamming of radars.

After the war, world wide research in astronomy at radio wavelengths blossomed. In the United States an important site for such research was at the Naval Research Laboratory (NRL) located across the Potomac River near Washington, D.C. Nan writes in her autobiography that she "happened to be at the right place at the right time." That is modest and true, for she found herself living in a Washington suburb, Alexandria, with an interest and experience in astronomy, and a job at NRL—she was on her way to becoming a notable radio astronomer. Her first paper (1952) was on solar radiation; following publications were on radio sources and on 21 cm spectral line observations. In 1955 she entered the graduate astronomy program at Harvard focusing on 21 cm extragalactic hydrogen studies. Her dissertation was on the local group spiral galaxy M33.

After receiving her Ph.D. Nan continued her study of nearby galaxies using the Harvard 60-foot antenna equipped with the world's most sensitive radio astronomy system, a maser amplifier built by John Jelley and Brian Cooper. IC342 was one of the galaxies Nan observed. She derived its neutral hydrogen content and total mass using the strength and velocity range of its 21 cm line radiation. For this calculation she also needed a distance to this galaxy. For other galaxies she had studied, e.g. M33 and M101, distance estimates were available from optical studies. Less was known about the distance of IC342 because of its low galactic latitude and hence large and uncertain foreground obscuration. Its radial velocity is also low, making a reshift-distance estimate very uncertain. Edwin Hubble discusses this galaxy in his classic book "*The Realm of the Nebulae.*" Nan used her 21 cm derived data to estimate a distance—this is a precursor to and a decade before the Tully-Fisher relation widely used today to estimate galaxy distances.

Nan is best known for her pioneering work in Milky Way spectral line research at the Radio Astronomy Laboratory of the University of California at Berkeley. Her personal account: interactions and collaborations, questions and serendipity make fascinating reading. Future historians of science piecing together the first decades of radio astronomy will note among her many accomplishments her work on high velocity hydrogen clouds, on maser-excited OH emission, and the discovery of compact, very small neutral hydrogen features in the interstellar medium. And to further help those future historians let me note what doesn't come across in a scientific paper, Nan's warmth and charm. She is a marvelous person, and an outstanding astronomer.

Morton S. Roberts
National Radio Astronomy Observatory
Charlottesville, VA
March 2006

FOREWORD: THE WOMAN IN THE WOMAN SCIENTIST

By any benchmark you care to choose, Nan Dieter Conklin's professional achievements are impressive. She helped pioneer a new science, radio astronomy; along with her discoveries of new small-scale gas cloud structures in the vast depths between stars, she also, in a moment of dizzying serendipity, found that the interstellar gas changed on a hitherto inconceivably rapid scale. This, her story of her life and work, should command interest simply as the memoir of a significant scientist—exactly as would that of an Edwin Hubble or an Edward Barnard. And so it does. But it is undeniable that her story also commands interest of another sort: because she was a woman who nevertheless pursued and succeeded in science—the first U.S. woman whose Ph.D. thesis was based on her own radio astronomy research and the first U.S. woman to publish original radio astronomy research in a refereed journal—and because she lived and worked with the degenerative disease multiple sclerosis, MS.

No scientist really wants to be looked at through the viewfinder window labeled "woman scientist". After all, the whole point of science is that the unique personal characteristics of the individual scientist have no influence on the outcomes of their work. Moreover, if the ideal is that one day the numbers will be so close to even that no one will even notice if a scientist is male or female (or black or white, etc. etc.), then admiring a scientist for her gender can ironically perpetuate the expectation that women scientists are an unusual breed. (And if this is true about gender, in this memoir Nan makes the same point only more firmly with respect to her illness. She is very clear that it has been crucial to her survival that she be treated and regarded as normal and not be admired through a viewfinder window marked "disabled".)

Yet at the same time these issues will not go away. At the time when Nan began her scientific research there were young women who were, subtly or explicitly, turned away from science, and when her story is read tomorrow there will be other young women, hard put to it to name a woman scientist apart from Marie Curie, still wondering and doubting if science is a possibility for them. There will, alas, also be people who, newly diagnosed with some debilitating condition, darkly imagine the beginning of their ends. Nan's life is part of bigger stories, about women in science and about people who struggle with chronic disease, and her memoirs tell us something more about those stories. Conversely, knowing something about these bigger stories can help us as readers understand something more about the life-story she presents to us here. So for readers unfamiliar with the "woman question in science" I will briefly sketch here something of the historical context in which Nan began her career.

As historian Margaret Rossiter has documented in two impeccably researched, detailed volumes, it is true that overall women have confronted many barriers to their having careers in science, unfortunately especially in the USA where many institutions and the national culture were overtly hostile to their involvement. Most of these barriers still exist. Women confronted two forms of discrimination: (1) direct or overt discrimination, in which men actively objected to women's involvement in science or in which women were seen and treated differently because they were women and (2) "structural" discrimination, a series of social mechanisms that have resulted in women remaining almost entirely clustered in lower ranking, lower paid jobs in science, and in some areas of science and not others. The first kind of discrimination is the less common; the second kind, being nobody's fault and in fact often apparently supported by women's own choices, is by far the most challenging to overcome.

There are a number of factors that generate structural discrimination in science, resulting in girls and women moving out of scientific careers in every age group. In childhood, girls lack role models and images of women as scientists: scientists tend to be portrayed as male, and as having characteristics that are found undesirable in females: poor grooming, poor social skills and so forth. Differences in treatment and expectations at home and at school tend to result in boys getting more scientific and technical experience and encouragement to pursue those experiences. Let us not forget that until the 1950s, many girls didn't get any education in the "hard" sciences at all, nor were most ever able to even dream of tertiary education, which was expensive and often reserved for sons. (Tertiary education is still not even dreamed of by the less privileged in American society, among whom we can only guess are many who would make fine scientists.) At university, women students can be put off by boisterous masculine classroom cultures and laboratory environments, and suffer from a lack of mentoring and exclusion from informal social networks among scientists in comparison with their male peers. When they graduate and enter research careers, they tend to be given research projects and jobs that are more labour intensive, depend more on routine repetition, and are less theoretically adventurous. Or they are expected to perform jobs that are effectively treated as "women's work", like cataloguing specimens or managing reference materials, along with making coffee.

And so women's disadvantage accumulates. With more labor intensive research they publish less; with more routine experimentation at the core of their work they publish in lower impact journals; and so they attract less grant money and fewer accolades, and so they are less likely be regarded as a bold, brilliant young researcher on whom professorial attention is to be lavished, and so they are promoted less ... and so by almost imperceptible degrees the bright young ambitious student becomes a self-effacing modest woman scientist, almost invisible in the pages of scientific history. And this is without reckoning with the family duties that women scientists typically have had in a much greater degree than their male counterparts—looking after elderly parents if not a husband and children.

This structural discrimination has resulted in a quite powerful and long lasting stereotype about women scientists, which unfortunately coloured many senior men's perception of what they were like. Here's a typical example, from an article titled *"Women in Physics and Chemistry"* published in the Electrochemical Society Journal of August 1954.

> *"Women are most successful and appear happiest in the position of technical aide to scientists and engineers engaged in research and development programs. They are more willing than men to do routine, repetitious work. They are patient, faithful and dexterous. They are subjective rather than objective in attitude. They get satisfaction in the approbation of colleagues ..."*

So, although admiring their dedication (and being grateful for their retiring modesty), women scientists were seen as less intellectually "bold" than men, less adventurous, less creative in their thinking, less capable of leadership. In this way structural discrimination sets up expectations that tend to reinforce that discrimination.

At the time Nan began her career, towards the end of World War II, attitudes were somewhat nastier even than this. Women scientists were denounced as emotionally unstable, blamed for difficulties with other faculty women, criticized as poor risks who would marry soon and leave, or else become crazy old maids if they did not, and who would certainly become bitter and unpleasant to work with when they were inevitably not promoted. I will leave it to the reader to trace something of these attitudes in Nan's story. As you will find, Nan faced both direct and structural discrimination. When she was a student women were still fighting to be even eligible for faculty jobs at most American research institutions (other than women's colleges, which had limited means for funding research anyway). After 300 years Harvard's Faculty of Arts and Sciences, where Nan did her Ph.D., had only just tenured a woman – in Byzantine art. As a matter of fact—and this anecdote may serve to illustrate how widespread discrimination was for Nan's contemporaries—it took money and not merely scientific brilliance to change this situation: the second woman was tenured as a result of a bequest made in 1947 by a man whose son was killed in the war and whose daughter was a Radcliffe alumnae and anthropologist. (The search committee considered astronomer Cecilia Payne-Gaposchkin, Nan's mentor, for the endowed professorship, but the job eventually went to an historian).

And Nan was trying to enter the most masculine of all the sciences – physics. (An aside: the reasons for women's remarkably and continually low participation rates in physics compared with other sciences are complex. Crucial factors include the particularly competitive and boisterous masculine workplace culture of physics in America (luckily for Nan, radio astronomy turned out to be more female-friendly than other fields of physics) and the especially high cultural status that physics held among the sciences for most of the twentieth century, which seemed to reserve it to men. What does not explain low female participation rates in physics is female biology, such as different structures in male and female brains resulting from different hormonal production in early life, the current version of this very old theory. Readers interested in biological differences in the capacity of males and females to do science should use the select bibliography offered at the end of this volume.)

In 1946 there were 900 women physicists in America, which sounds like a lot but which made up just 4.9 percent of the total. The 100 female astronomers made up 16.6 percent of the total. Although there had been some call for women to take up "men's jobs" in science in war time, Margaret Rossiter discovered that prevailing attitudes that saw women as fit solely for supporting roles meant that only exceptional women scientists really benefited as a result of the war. In any case by 1948 the percentages had fallen to 2.6 and 9.9 percent respectively as a result of a policy of pushing out women students and employees in order to favour male war veterans. And whilst research funding for the hard sciences expanded enormously during the Cold War, America also experienced a resurgence of a strongly pro-natalist ideology that saw women's place as firmly in the home, being good mothers. In 1954 women made up just 3 percent of physicists and astronomers, and this rose only half a percent by 1972. During these decades pretty much all women scientists were paid significantly less than men.

Under these circumstances it is reasonable for the reader to be impressed with Nan's ability to do the science she did—let alone with her ability to undertake research of international quality and still raise her children, for many years without the help of grandparents or partner. In fact it raises another question, namely why—since merit alone was far from enough to grant women scientists professional equality in America—was Nan able to be as successful a scientist as she was? A good part of the answer lies in three simple factors. (1) She had the good fortune to work in a department well known to be influenced not only by an outstanding woman scientist (Payne-Gaposchkin), but by a man who was highly sympathetic to women (Bart Bok). Harvard produced more female astronomers than any other institution in this era. (2) Because of this, she was able to create strong peer networks that generated job opportunities, professional support and full access to information. And (3) Her timing was brilliant. She embarked on an entirely new science (radio astronomy) right at its beginning, when exciting discoveries were made daily and when trained personnel were in demand, giving her maximum opportunity to play an important role and minimising the possibilities of getting quietly directed towards some form of 'women's work'. Of course, all of this worked only because Nan was clearly not only very talented but also incredibly hard working. (The reader may like to speculate also on personality traits they detect in these memoirs that may also have helped—though I am bound to say that highly successful women scientists have had very varied personalities and working styles. Some are more collegial, consensus-based and team focused—qualities western women scientists are often expected to have—and others are individualistic and dogmatic-qualities detected, without admiration, in Japanese women physicists by their male peers.)

Nan does not much discuss the "woman scientist" issue in this memoir, though she is aware throughout that it exists. By and large she was not forced by ugly attitudes or circumstances to be much conscious of her gender when among her peers, and in this she is similar to most other successful women scientists. But that doesn't mean that gender didn't nonetheless colour every aspect of her life. Nan doesn't just write here as a scientist "who happened to be a woman", but very much "as a woman who happened to be a scientist" (to use her own words). The way she tells her story reveals her gender as a central organising principle of her life and identity in a way that is very different from the autobiographical writing of male scientists. What great male scientist would ever say, as Nan does here, that marriage could fulfill many of the emotional needs formerly satisfied by science, or who would relinquish science to give their all to marriage, even if pressed by the constraints of illness, as she was? For which such scientist-autobiographer would the problems and vagaries of family life act as such a determining factor in the geography and pattern of his career? Which would agonise, as she hints she did, about the costs his children bore from his working life?

These memoirs are a mix of great frankness and immense privacy and are notable almost as much for what Nan doesn't discuss as much as for what she does. (How, for example, did the many articles viciously attacking women scientists as poor mothers that were published during those years make her feel?) Any form of autobiography is actually a kind of fabrication—a making of the self according to the author's needs and beliefs at the time of writing, a lens that guides the choice and framing of scenes from the past. The interested reader may find that, however much Nan's science was free from gender, her life-writing shows many of the same traits identified in the works of other women autobiographers, such as her tendency to define herself in relation to the important Others in her life (astronomy, her husband). Such a reader may also care to explore Nan's illness narrative and compare it with those of others, or to explore the non-scientific themes that pervade the work, such as her continual counterpoint to science, artistic discovery.

This memoir, then, has much to offer to readers desirous of tracing the effects of gender, narrative, illness, and self-representation in science, and this foreward merely presents a toolbox sufficient to begin such endeavours. I would only add that a close reading will reveal what I as editor was privileged to discover in more depth—it is not every elderly lady who can stand a stranger monkeying with her memories, let alone put aside emotion to join the process—the professionalism, pride, piquancy and stubborn strength in Nan. Her experiences were out of the common way (who among us, not a billionaire, goes to live in Menorca?!) and are still vividly fresh as she describes them on the page. But to me she chiefly embodies the virtues that I have found to be common among women scientists of her generation: clear sighted devotion to the unworldly goal of gaining knowledge, a great capacity for pleasure and delight in the natural world and in the creative endeavours of others, almost innocently regardless of social prejudices like race, nationality or creed. And a distinct lack of capacity for angst or for suffering fools gladly. If bigger stories make her memoirs interesting, it is these qualities that make it a pleasure to read, and I commend it to you.

Claire Hooker, Ph.D.
University of Toronto
January 2006

Three faces of Nan. Pastel by Jade Fon, 1969.

TIMELINE

June 10, 1926	Born Nannielou Reier, to Paul Reier (salesman, b. 1897) and Alice Henderson Reier (homemaker, b. 1901), Springfield, Illinois
1928	Family moved to St. Louis
1934	Family moved to Baltimore
Fall 1944	Entered Goucher college in Baltimore
Fall 1945	Began first astronomy course
June 1947	Maria Mitchell fellowship, Nantucket Met Peter Hepburn
June 1948	Graduated Goucher college Engaged to Peter Maria Mitchell fellowship, Nantucket
Fall 1948	U.S. Coast and Geodetic Survey, mathematician
June 1950	Married Peter
March 1951	Naval Research Laboratory, astronomer
March 1951	Discovery of interstellar hydrogen by Ewen and Purcell
May 1951	Solar bursts observed at 8.5 mm
December 1951	Amy Wray Hepburn born
1952	First published paper
June 1953	Separated, moved to SE Washington, D.C.
1954	21 cm receiver activated at Naval Research Laboratory

1955	Married Carl Dieter Entered Harvard graduate program
April 1958	Earned Ph.D.
July 1958	Mary Nan Dieter born
Fall 1958	National Science Foundation Fellowship
1958	Air Force Cambridge Research Laboratory, astronomer
1959	First sign of MS
1960	MS diagnosed
March 1965	University of California, Berkeley, research astronomer Met Garret Conklin
1966	Discovery of anomalous OH
January 1968	Married Garret
April 1973	Fellowship to USSR
1975	Discovery of very small HI cloud
1975	Bought Paris apartment
1977	Retired from UC Berkeley to Menorca
1981	Moved to Vermont
1982	Sold Paris apartment
1996	First sign of Garret's Alzheimer's
1998	Moved to Seattle
April 1999	Moved to Northshore House
August 2002	Death of Garret
October 2003	Moved with Jenny to Brittany Park

INTRODUCTION

Why have I written this, the story of my life, and why do I imagine that anyone would read it? I began by writing a chronicle of my life in science, intended primarily as an historical document, that is now available at the National Radio Astronomy Observatory web site (*http://www.nrao.edu/archives/Conklin/ conklin.shtml*). Next I rewrote that chronicle to read to my creative writing group. Their most frequent questions and comments all centered on one theme: "But how did you feel about it? And why did you decide to do this or that? Make it more personal!" Eventually they urged me to write the whole story, and so I did.

I shall include much of my life in astronomy, but with an attempt to make it accessible to the general reader. That part of the story has a major theme of its own—the number of times I happened to be at the right place at the right time. The early days of any branch of science are likely to be filled with drama, and radio astronomy was no exception. And there were other ways in which my life might be considered unusual: I received my doctorate from Harvard in April 1958, before "feminism" was a part of the national language, and in 1960 I was diagnosed with multiple sclerosis, MS. I was fortunate in that the collection of symptoms I experienced—including an unsteadiness in walking and a tendency to grow extremely weary, often unpredictably—did not rule my life. In fact, none of my professional colleagues knew that I was sick or handicapped in any way. MS did catch up with me eventually, but since I can see and hear and think it still does not dominate my life.

In addition to doing the work I loved, I eventually found a man to share my life. I have enjoyed writing about our marriage, and hope these words will bring Garret alive to the reader. I have tried to show what our marriage meant to both of us. Perhaps I can convey a little of the feeling that it was always, under any circumstances, better to be together than apart. Any home we made anywhere was a refuge for us both and a place of calm and warmth for visitors. We shared so much—in places like San Francisco Bay, France, the Soviet Union, Menorca, and rural Vermont. Every new home was an opportunity for me to create a beautiful background, and for Garret to invent ways to make it work efficiently. Our house was always filled with music. It was the nearest thing to a "marriage made in heaven," hence *Two Paths to Heaven's Gate.*

To say that I have written these words is not quite accurate, because I have actually spoken them and computer magic has transformed them to the printed word. The process appears to give the story an air of telling rather than composing. Throughout I shall be as truthful as I can, but I am recalling events through the prism of imperfect memory. Also I must protect the innocent (and sometimes the guilty) people who have touched my life.

1944 – 1965

GOUCHER, 1944-1948

In many ways my life began not in 1926, the date on my birth certificate, but in 1944 when I entered Goucher College. My early years, of course, were full of vital and formative events, but somehow the doors that opened before me as a freshman set me free to find and follow dreams. I suppose that's what any education aims to do.

I had hoped to go away to school, but there was not the money for room and board, so I became a "city girl": I lived at home in Baltimore with my mother and father, took advantage of scholarships for tuition, and worked at various jobs to pay for my books.

At the time the campus was in the heart of downtown Baltimore in Victorian buildings with the air of scholarly pursuits long practiced. Here I could throw myself headlong into learning, and, incidentally, avoid the baffling problems of being a teenage girl. Since this was 1944 most young men were away in the service, and for many girls dates consisted of dancing under the watchful eye of the USO (translation for the very young—an organization that provided chaperoned fun for the boys away from home). One bright spot in the social calendar was the opportunity to spend a weekend at Annapolis. The Naval Academy there was dazzling and the young men uniformly handsome in their uniforms, but my reactions resembled more those of a frightened rabbit than a sophisticated socialite. I was more at ease with books.

I had decided in high school that science was what I wanted to do. But both physics and chemistry required extensive lab work, and I was absolutely no good at that. Math seemed to be the answer. However, although I could do the problems and pass the tests, I could not imagine doing anything truly creative. My adviser, Dr. Marian Torrey, told me of a new course to be offered in the department, elementary astronomy, taught by a woman who was a graduate of Goucher, Dr. Helen Dodson. Helen (as I came to know her) was doing her own solar research at the University of Michigan—unusual for a woman, to say the least. At just this time she decided that she would like a break (I never knew quite why) and came back to her alma mater to teach.

And teach she did. For example, one of the first projects she proposed amazed us all. We were to pick a place from which we could see the sunrise or sunset about once a week, and to sketch the horizon-line including trees or buildings. Each week we were to locate against this background the point at which the sun rose or set. During our ten-week course the point of sunrise changed over a wide angle, something I'd never noticed before. I continue to be aware of the sun's position as a measure of the seasons—and that was 60 years ago!

After two weeks in that first astronomy course I knew I had found what I wanted. Helen was more than a teacher; she was the living proof that it <u>could</u> be done, a woman doing her own research in a field I longed to enter. Her stories of working with Bernard Lyot, who was perfecting his revolutionary new device, the coronagraph, were tantalizing. Lyot's invention would mimic a solar eclipse by blocking out the bright disc of the Sun in order to photograph the Sun's faint outer atmosphere without waiting for an eclipse. And her description of his observatory on the Pic du Midi in the Pyrenees and her journey on skis to reach it only added a touch of magic. When I learned that she sometimes <u>sailed</u> across Lake Angeles to reach the observatory in Ann Arbor, I imagined myself commuting at the tiller of a tiny sailboat and was lost (or rather, found!)

First, though, I had some hurdles to jump. During the first two years at Goucher a student could take almost any courses she wanted, with the understanding that at the end of the sophomore year there would be a large, general examination in all areas included in a liberal arts education. Each student was expected in the next year to take courses in her weak subjects. One of mine was art, and so I took a class in charcoal drawing without much enthusiasm. Although I was not very good at it, I thought I might come back to it some day. Another deficiency was philosophy. I found Greek philosophy a colossal bore, but was able to manage by choosing mathematics in Plato's philosophy as the topic for my paper. Now, of course, I remember not a word of it!

There was one further requirement for graduation that I was not at all sure I could fulfill. I must swim ten lengths of the pool with at least two of them in the Australian crawl, and I must stay afloat for ten minutes without touching the sides or bottom of the pool. I remember vividly the oppressive heat, powerful chlorine smell, and the odd distortion of sound in that room. Well, obviously, I did it, but only with the utmost determination. Helen protested, "You can't know that you want to make astronomy your career without some experience of the real thing," and she set about finding me the chance to get it. For the summers of 1947 and 1948 I was awarded fellowships to the Maria Mitchell Observatory on the beautiful island of Nantucket. I discovered many things there—not all of them astronomical.

NANTUCKET, SUMMERS OF 1947 & 1948

The journey began by train to Woods Hole on Cape Cod and then by ferry to Martha's Vineyard and Nantucket, thirty miles at sea. As we sailed into the large harbor I saw a place utterly different from anything I had ever seen. The docks and small, neat buildings on the wharf spoke of another time. One could imagine a whaling ship coming home to this safe haven after a long and dangerous voyage, and in a strange way I felt that I, too, was coming home. (It's odd, but remembering this time more than half a century later leaves me longing for something I have lost—perhaps youth and this perfect place.) Margaret Harwood, the director of the Observatory and the very picture of an elderly New England lady, met the ferry and took me to her small cottage in the town. She served me the perfect meal of New England quahog chowder and her own beach plum jam in a room rich with dark wood and a beautiful lamp that pulled down from the ceiling.

Miss Harwood's cottage was a few steps across the grass from the Maria Mitchell Observatory, a low brick building with a dome at one end. Maria Mitchell had been born on Nantucket in 1818 and became the first woman astronomer in this country. Encouraged by her father who was also an astronomer, she made many meaningful contributions to the science, including the discovery of a comet. As professor of astronomy at Vassar, she encouraged young women to follow their dreams. Just beyond along the lane was Maria Mitchell's tiny house (now a historical museum), and across the lane the Lydia S. Hinchman house where I was to stay. All these houses were covered with wood shingles weathered by the salt air to the soft, dove gray of so many buildings on the island. The cluster of buildings seemed, above all, tidy. All of them (plus a library of more recent vintage) were maintained as part of the Hinchman Foundation for Natural History that supported research in astronomy, biology, and botany—all as part of the heritage of Nantucket. I shared the fine old house with three other women who spent the summer working on the island under fellowships in the life sciences.

The next morning I walked across the lane to learn about my job, and to meet the other fellowship student with whom I would share duties. Wray MacKay was a Nantucket high school senior who was about as nervous as I was. Miss Harwood did nothing to calm our fears; rather, she made it clear that she expected us to carry out her instructions precisely. She loved the observatory and intended to protect it from careless young people. Wray and I learned that our duties would include photographing star fields through the observatory's 7.5" refracting telescope on any clear night when the moon was not too bright. The photographs were made on 8 x 10 glass plates that the observer was to develop during the night. The plates were stored in closed, polished wooden cabinets intended to preserve them, but even so we needed to wash all of them occasionally to remove salt-spray. (I had awful visions of dropping one.)

Our principal work lay in the study of stars that vary in brightness. Some of the stars change over a period of days; others, over hours or minutes. Our small telescope made it necessary to use long exposures (usually one hour) to detect faint stars. That, of course, ruled out study of the very interesting stars that changed brightness in less than an hour. Lesson #1 in fitting the study to the equipment!

After choosing several variable stars of interest, we used the coordinates of a reasonably bright star near the center of the field to set up the telescope and begin the exposure. The guidance mechanism of the telescope was very good, but not accurate enough to produce perfect round stellar images over such a long exposure. The only way to get them was to keep the central star precisely on cross-hairs in the eyepiece by moving the telescope a little, very little, with a hand-held manual control. The quality and vigilance of the observer's control were apparent in the shape of the final images.

The demands of becoming an extension of the telescope's guidance system did not prevent my being aware of the pure beauty of the night sky. Nantucket is thirty miles at sea, and a clear night there has a quality that is both indescribable and unforgettable. I became aware for the first time of the sweep of the stars across the sky from dusk to dawn. I was amazed at how often I had to move the slit of the telescope's dome to keep up. Hard to believe that the majesty of the motion results from a simple thing like the rotation of the earth.

After a plate was developed, the next step was to identify an image of a star varying in brightness with time. It was often a known variable but one for which neither the amplitude (amount) nor the period (duration) of the variation had been determined. The brightness of the star on our new plate was compared with that on earlier ones—hence the need for those perfect round images. The process was a good deal more tedious than it sounds, but it was a thrill (albeit a small one) to find the time interval that was the period of a regularly varying star.

It was, after all, new. This was Helen's "real thing," and it was all I had hoped it would be.

The work left a lot of time to explore the island, especially since I had many afternoons free. I found a beautiful, sandy beach on the sheltered side of the island, quite close enough to reach on my bicycle. Many times, particularly in June, there was no one else there. Because Nantucket lies just on the edge of the Gulf stream, the water is much warmer than on the mainland beaches. Summer temperatures rarely reach higher than 75 degrees, and clear days are as breathtaking as the nights.

My room in Hinchman house was cozy with a fireplace (that I tried once). My companions and I often had meals together either in the very spacious kitchen or the more formal dining room. The fireplace there made this room warm and comfortable, and occasionally exciting. Not long before, some of the old shakes that covered the building had been replaced, making wonderful, dry firewood with old copper nails providing occasional fireworks. Most of the first floor of the house, however, was used for displays of Nantucket birds and wildflowers and for classes to study them. My friends were up before dawn to go bird-watching and to gather wildflowers in the cool of the morning. It was great to have the flowers in the house, in fact, a privilege. As elsewhere, picking wildflowers was forbidden, with heather at the top of the forbidden list, but the authorities had made an exception for our nature classes. And these women were serious birdwatchers, as I discovered when I went along on one early-morning trek.

About two weeks after I arrived Wray's older brother, Peter Hepburn, came to the observatory. He was a sophomore at Georgetown University in Washington D.C., not too far from Baltimore. For the summer he was living with his mother and brother and sister, and driving the taxi for the Seacliff Inn Hotel. Our brief conversation did not prepare me for what I found on my desk several days later. There was a package made up of a note wrapped around a tiny bouquet of wild blue asters, a flower that must have been picked very early in the morning. The note from Peter was an invitation to the movies the following evening! Since part of his duty with the taxi was to meet the early boat from the mainland, he was up and about quite early enough to pick the flowers—an unforgettable romantic beginning. We spent many happy days together exploring the moors and beaches and sharing our lives and dreams.

One of our first days we went to the lighthouse at Sconset at the other end of the island. It lies atop a 100 foot cliff above the sea that on this day was covered with daisies. I learned that Peter had been in the Navy for two years as a radioman on a destroyer in the Pacific. He didn't talk about that time, then or ever, but his memories must have been vivid, because in quiet moments he often tapped something in Morse code with his foot. Unfortunately, I was never able to decode it.

Kay-tee, Peter's mother, and Kit, his sister, welcomed me into their warm, and lively family. During the winter they and Wray lived in a beautiful house in Nantucket town that became too expensive in the summer. Every summer they moved to a tiny house (called the Bobstay) in the middle of a hay field. It consisted of two small buildings—one a living room-kitchen and the other, bedroom. The whole was quite like living on a small boat. Kay-tee was a splendid cook, and we spent many evenings together—especially lovely when the scent of new-mown hay filled the house. It all seemed quite magical to me, because I had never had such times with my own family, and because Peter was the first young man who really paid attention to me.

Near the end of the summer ladies of Hinchman house invited Peter to dinner. One of them, Miss Rice, taught me how to make my first blueberry pie, beginning with picking the wild low-bush berries. We laid a fire in the dining room, and set a festive table. The appointed time came and went. Our guest never arrived or called. (I now forget why—the excuse wasn't sufficient.) Miss Rice must have grown weary of my whining about the whole thing, because she taught me a valuable lesson. She said, "Nan, are you ever going to forgive him?" She saw the answer on my face, and added, "Well, then, why not now?"

U.S. COAST AND GEODETIC SURVEY, 1948-1951

At the end of the summer of 1947 I returned for my senior year at Goucher College in Baltimore, and Peter for his sophomore year at Georgetown in Washington D.C. He came on many weekends to stay with us. It was great fun for us both, even though it was obvious my parents did not like him, especially my father. Dad seemed to find countless petty ways to make his feelings clear, which of course only made me more determined to follow my heart. On the day of my graduation Peter and I were engaged to be married, and we returned to Nantucket for another summer.

It was a summer to remember for a lifetime, but near the end of it I was forced to make an agonizing decision. One afternoon standing in our hayfield Peter told me that he wanted to go to the Episcopal theological seminary in Alexandria, Virginia, and to follow a career in the church. I was astonished for several reasons. First of all, I had expected Peter to write, using his unique imagination and clever, sometimes rather sharp wit. Then there was the inescapable conclusion that I would be a clergyman's wife—not something I had ever imagined. I did not see how I could combine astronomy and this marriage. For the time being I went along with it, hoping the future would sort things out.

In the fall of 1948 I found a job with the title of mathematician (!) in the Astronomy and Geodesy Section of the U.S. Coast and Geodetic Survey in Washington, D.C. I was glad to find a job in Washington because Peter would be there, and because I wanted to move away from home. The job was very much entry-level but I was glad to get it. The Survey used observations of the position of stars to establish precise locations for their primary benchmarks. I entered data from the field into a system of well-established formulas to derive these locations.

In other words, I filled out stacks of forms. Not quite what I had in mind. However, I did learn about the discipline of a real job and about how much of any job, even in science, is made up of dull, demanding hours. But then, my desk was in the Commerce Department at 14th and Pennsylvania Avenue in the Nation's Capital. It was a perfect city for the young and poor: parks and monuments and libraries and museums—all free and safe.

It is a strange part of life that one occasionally has experiences that remain in the memory long after others have vanished. One project that I worked on at the Coast and Geodetic Survey provided such a haunting memory. The research project was, "Are there tides in the solid earth like those in the oceans?" They would of course be very much smaller in amplitude and difficult to detect. In fact, the designers of the experiment required extraordinary measures to ensure that the measurements would be entirely free of factors that could be confused with true "earth tides." They chose an isolated room deep under the Commerce Department for the location of the high-precision pendulum on which the observations would depend. I was one of the workers who spent 12 hour days watching over this somewhat spooky experiment.

I guess the experiment was not actually "spooky," but the absolute quiet was. I sat in a bare room, just big enough for a small chair and table, with no windows and no apparent contact with the outside world. Every half-hour I opened the heavy door into a larger room where a pendulum, housed in a glass case, continued to swing slowly back and forth. As I remember it, the only other equipment was a small seismograph recording a thin red ink line on the slowly moving paper tape. In the absolute stillness it was all hypnotic. I don't remember the sort of measurements I recorded or the outcome of the experiment, but I do remember the hours I spent in the small room reading Arnold Bennett's *The Old Wives' Tale*.

As the time for Peter's graduation approached, June 1950, we began to plan our wedding. We wanted it to be at the church in downtown Washington where we had made many friends, but my parents wanted it in Baltimore. When I insisted, they said they would not come. I somehow managed to pay for quite a simple celebration that, however, included a white bridal gown and a reception in the church hall. At the last minute my parents decided to come, and my father escorted me down the aisle to the sound of the stirring wedding march. I was not prepared for the flood of emotion that poured over me when the minister began to read the meltingly beautiful marriage service from the *Book of Common Prayer*. I quietly wept during the whole thing to the gentle amusement of my groom.

Peter had been accepted at the seminary, and after a honeymoon in Nantucket we were able to move into an apartment quite beyond our means, because several apartments in the Parkfairfax section of Alexandria were rented to seminarians at a reduced rate. Its attractive brick buildings, each made up of six apartments with private entrances, lay along the winding roads of the hilly area. Ours, on the second floor, was a delightful place to make our first home. As I think back on it, I can't remember how we did all this on my modest salary. It certainly included bookcases made of bricks and boards, and many tuna casseroles. This is where the fairy tale would have it, "and they lived happily ever after." Well, not quite.

NAVAL RESEARCH LABORATORY, 1951-1955

As I was waking to the reality of my new marriage I grew more dissatisfied with my job in the Commerce Department. Continuing my education at the moment was out of the question, but I could not give up hope of doing something in astronomy. And then one Sunday in March of 1951 I saw an amazing picture in the newspaper. It showed a large (50 ft) dish antenna on the roof of a building at the Naval Research Laboratory, a major facility just across the Potomac River from Alexandria. The final wedge-shaped section of the antenna was just being lowered into place. I knew that there had been observations of the sun's emission at radio wavelengths with such an antenna. Perhaps this was my opportunity. I discovered that not only was it planned to do "radio astronomy" with it, but there was no one at NRL with as much knowledge of astronomy as I had, small though that was. So I was hired! The men who were planning to use the antenna had the vision to see that their understanding of electronics gained in the development of radar during the war could be useful in the new branch of astronomy. I knew nothing of electronics, but apparently I could bring something useful to the group.

To my delight I found that I could "sail" to work. Well, it wasn't quite sailing. NRL had a small motor launch (manned by U.S. Navy sailors, no less) to ferry workers across the Potomac from Alexandria. It ran summer and winter in the best Naval tradition; I especially remember very windy winters.

Finding this job was a truly extraordinary piece of luck. NRL was one of the very few places in the United States where what was becoming known as "radio astronomy" was being pursued. The U.S. Navy perhaps seems an unlikely group to be investigating a new discipline in astronomy, but at this point it was electronic equipment that made it possible at all. The Naval research facilities had a wealth of experience in developing and perfecting radar instruments and they need only concentrate not on transmitting radio waves (as in radar) but receiving them from "radio sources."

Incidentally, although this was the male-dominated U.S. Navy in 1951, I felt my male colleagues had no hesitation in working with a young woman.

The years I worked at NRL were full of variety and surprises. When I first arrived the equipment was not ready and I busied myself in translating French astronomical articles. Again not what I had in mind, but useful at least to me. By early summer, however, Dr. John Hagen, director of the section, put into operation his equipment to record radio radiation from the sun at a wavelength of 8.5mm. This very short wavelength provided a new window through which to observe objects beyond the earth; it was shorter than any so far used.

Radio telescopes work in pretty much the same way as optical ones. The great reflectors like the 200 inch telescope on Mt. Palomar gather light from the sky, and in the same way the radio antennas gather radio waves from the sky. The only difference lies in the wavelength observed. The wavelength of light is much shorter than the wavelengths in the radio spectrum, and this leads to two differences in their reception. Short-wavelength light is collected effectively by telescopes measured in inches rather than feet, but those reflectors must have very, very precise glass surfaces. Longer wavelength radio waves require much larger "mirrors" like the 50 foot antenna at NRL, but they can be made of metal with much less precise surfaces. In both cases the larger the collector, the more radiation collected, and the finer the distinction between two sources close together in the sky (called beam width in radio astronomy). There are other differences in details in the way the data is handled, and the devil is definitely in those details.

The antenna we used to observe the Sun was only two feet in diameter, but when coupled with a very sensitive receiver, ideal for our purpose. Since we planned to record radio radiation from the whole disc of the Sun at once, we did not need a large reflector. We recorded the entire 8.5 mm radiation from the Sun throughout the day in order to detect any sudden increase in its intensity.

Such sudden increases, though amounting to an exceedingly small percentage of the sun's total radiation, could yield new insight into our understanding of the sun. They had been observed at longer wavelengths and occurred near the time of the large solar flares that had been observed optically. Each burst was characterized by a rapid rise in intensity and a slower fall. We discovered bursts of radiation on five occasions between May 1 and October 1 (resulting in my first published paper!)[1].

While I was having a splendid time at work, things were falling apart at home. In the spring of 1951 officials at the seminary had asked Peter to leave the school, and suggested that he see a psychoanalyst. I was shocked and bewildered. I knew that Peter was disturbed about something, but I had no idea it was so profound. He began the treatment, bringing further drain on our meager resources, and with no noticeable result. The worst part for me was that I must not ask, "Is it a help?" or "What's happening?" During this time Peter made some money by driving a taxi in Washington, and to my delight, said that he had submitted a short story to the Atlantic Monthly, but did not want me to read it until it was actually published. One memorable day in June I discovered both that I was pregnant and that there really was no short story. It had been a lie. Sometimes I think Peter was uncertain of the difference between fantasy and reality. But the baby was distinctly real. The greatest difficulty with the pregnancy was my new distaste for coffee, including the smell of it. Mornings at the Naval facility were difficult, but a refuge nevertheless.

On December 4, 1951 Amy Wray (for Peter's brother) was born, all 5lbs 2oz of her, and nothing was ever quite the same again. Her small size and consequent small stomach made the first weeks very hard on me, but she was the miracle that all new babies are—and she was mine. I needed to find a way to care for her and at the same time to make money at the job I loved. Of course, there were no day-care centers and no recognition that a new mother might need and want a career of her own. Fortunately, I found Annie Mahoney, who both looked and acted the part of a loving, patient Mammy. Her devotion to Amy was immediate and survived a morning when the little dear expressed her distaste for baby-food eggs by blowing a mouthful at her. Annie was a source of security for Amy through the changes that were to come.

Meantime, a major development was occurring in radio astronomy. At Harvard H.I.(Doc) Ewen completed his thesis with Dr. Edward Purcell, a Nobel laureate. Since they knew that neutral hydrogen atoms in the right conditions emitted radiation at a wavelength of 21 cm (in the radio part of the spectrum), and that those conditions existed in the gas that lies between the stars, they looked for it there. Since hydrogen is the most abundant element in the universe, and since its detection in the interstellar gas would provide astronomers with a powerful tool to study this gas, they and the astronomical community were delighted when in 1951 they found it[2].

The gas between the stars had been studied only by observing how it absorbs starlight. One trouble with this is that the number of directions in which the gas could be observed was limited to the direction of suitable stars. A second limitation is that the elements that show up in the optical range are rare compared to hydrogen.

Finding a way to detect the interstellar gas' major constituent opened the prospect of examining how much gas there is, how it moves, and how it relates to the structure of our galaxy. It was a stunning discovery. For me exploring those possibilities filled a lifetime of research.

A sensitive receiver for 21 cm wavelength was developed for our 50 foot dish. The intent was to make an extensive study of hydrogen clouds in interstellar space. But first John Hagen, Ed McClain and I (as a very junior partner) decided to test the new instrument by looking at known "radio sources."[3] The term shows how little was known about the sources; it meant only something that emitted radio waves, not distinguishing between different types of objects (a region of hot ionized gas like the famous nebula in Orion and supernova remnants like the Crab Nebula). The sources emitted waves over a wide range of radio wavelengths, and we expected to detect them easily. Detection of the much fainter radiation from interstellar hydrogen would surely be much harder. However, in these early days of radio astronomy it seemed that every new observation yielded unexpected results—heady days indeed.

Unfortunately unexpected things were happening at home as well. We had continued to live in our "subsidized" apartment although Peter was no longer at the seminary. A close friend in the rental office had made that possible, but one day Patricia came to talk to me. She said that we would have to leave because someone had seen Peter shooting a BB gun out the window. At the same time he was spending many hours on the floor of the living room playing with his large and beautiful collection of lead soldiers. (I guess Peter's erratic behavior was a product of early childhood experiences that he was never able to clarify.)

All this was clearly more than I could cope with. I no longer felt I could leave Amy with her father, not because he would ever dream of hurting her, but because he might forget his responsibility for her. At the end 1953 with heart-wrenching sadness Amy and I moved alone to a small, cheap apartment in D.C. My marriage was over. Peter essentially disappeared from our lives.

In the midst of this turmoil I had to go on working not only for the money but for the sake of my sanity. At the lab we began our survey of radio sources, and soon detected twenty sources, all but three of them associated with optically known objects. Two of those three were known from longer wavelength studies, but one remained a mystery. It was a complex source that we stumbled on and called cautiously NRL#9. I remember looking at its coordinates and having the feeling that they were familiar. Indeed they should have been. The source lay precisely in the direction of the center of our galaxy! What a joy it was to be able to contribute from my knowledge of astronomy! But another discovery awaited us. We decided to use the instrument efficiently—why not look at one of these radio sources and at the same time the interstellar hydrogen? We could do it by feeding the wide bandwidth signal from the source to one paper tape recorder and the narrow bandwidth signal from interstellar hydrogen to another. The antenna, of course, would be picking up different signals from the same patch of sky. The technique was to point the telescope near the source, move it through the position of the source and on beyond it. As the source came into view the ink line on the paper recorder went up as expected. I happened to be looking at the other recorder just as the ink line went down and said something like, "What's wrong? It went down." There was nothing wrong; the hydrogen gas was <u>absorbing</u> the radiation passing through it. Another first![4] The advantage of using the strong background source is that fainter hydrogen signals can be detected. It is, of course, analogous to the optical method for studying the interstellar gas by observing how it absorbs the background light of a star.

During the same period studies of the sun continued at NRL. In February 1952 there had been a total eclipse of the sun visible from Khartoum, Sudan, and an expedition had gone to observe it. (Although I could have left two-month old Amy with her father, I did not want to be away from her and so did not go along. Oddly enough, if I had gone I would have met Bernard Lyot, an old friend of Helen Dodson, my first teacher, and inventor of the coronagraph.) Though optical and radio observations continued, the eleven photographs of the solar corona that were taken there occupied many months of my time. The photographs were made on 8 x 10 plates (again) with a camera whose focal length was 18 feet. How this enormous camera was set up in the desert in the Sudan is a story in itself! As a result the image of the moon (blocking out the disc of the sun) was about two inches in diameter. The photographs made possible a photometric study of the whole inner corona.

I want to describe the scheme in some detail to give an idea of the magnitude of the task. A platform slightly less than two inches in diameter was added to a device for measuring the intensity of a small beam of light transmitted through the photographic image. With the image of the sun centered precisely on the platform it was rotated at a rate of about four minutes per rotation, while a pen recorder registered the changing intensity along a circle around the sun. All very clever, but not really necessary. When I began to analyze the data I realized that all I really needed was a series of measurements along a few selected radii, because it is the variation along such radii that yields information of use in understanding the corona. A model had been proposed for the corona that predicted a change in intensity along various radii, and my measurements substantiated that model, resulting in my first solo paper[5].

The experience of wasting so much time and effort by following someone else's direction convinced me that I wanted to direct my own work. It was not that I was sure I could avoid mistakes but that I wanted them to be my own. The only way to do that was to go to graduate school for the proper credentials. Another incident in connection with my paper on the solar corona emphasizes the less tangible value of self confidence (or arrogance?) that holding a graduate degree can bestow. A visiting astronomer (who will remain nameless) advised me to leave out of my paper my conclusion that material appeared to be flowing out through the coronal "streamers." I took the advice and came to wish I hadn't. Only later did I learn that I was right.

After we separated in 1953 Peter came to see Amy once. After that I never saw him again. Many years later, in the fall of 1961 when we were living in Lexington, Massachusetts, I got a surprise telephone call from Peter's brother, Wray. He said that Peter had been badly burned in a fire at the decrepit hotel in New York City where he had been living. He was only semi-conscious but had spoken my name. Wray called the next day to tell me Peter had died during the night and to ask if I would come to the funeral. Wray was planning to hold the service in the New York church where he was the minister, and invited me to stay in the rectory.

In the quiet, empty church the closed casket rested in front of the altar. My first thought was, "How long it is!"—but then he was 6 feet 1 inch tall. As I knelt there quietly weeping, I heard, "Nan, the last time we were together in front of an altar you wept, and now you're doing it again."

HARVARD, 1955-1958

In 1953 I faced the problems of a single mother in a time when there were few choices for child care. In fact, the term was unknown. Fortunately I made enough money to pay Annie to care for Amy, my two-year-old, at home. My memories of "home" can be characterized as bleak. Our apartment was part of a complex that included six buildings on a plot of land that probably had once been graced by growing, living things, but now struggled to support patches of forlorn grass. The area in SE Washington, closer to the lab (eliminating my boat ride), was certainly not poor, but lacked what might be called the "finer things of life." I learned there the importance to me of beauty and grace in my surroundings.

My constant source of nourishment lay, as it so often would, in my work, and in the people I worked with. The Naval Research Laboratory consisted of about twelve buildings aligned along two sides of a central grass mall behind a guarded entrance. Many different kinds of research were done there. On the floor below us was the Sound Laboratory, where scientists studied the propagation of sound in water (sonar). Their search for reliability in returned signals had some distinctly serendipitous effects. Much of the impetus for developing high fidelity in reproducing sound in air, that is for "high-fi" home music systems, came from their work. There was often loud, startling music filling the air of the building. One of the men most interested in reproducing classical music, Carl, became a friend. My experience in listening to classical music had been confined to radio broadcasts and 78rpm records, neither remotely high fidelity. The prospect of hearing music reproduced closer to the original performance was very appealing.

This time is particularly hard for me to recount with objectivity or even clarity. My handicap is that I know what happened later, and my memory is surely distorted because of it.

Carl and I had more in common than an interest in music. He was a great help in making me feel not entirely alone, especially with Amy. The three of us had good times together on our dreary little playground, and I was close to being happy. I had not given up the idea of graduate work in astronomy, and when two astronomers, Dr. Bart Bok and Dr. Richard Thomas, urged me to apply to Harvard, the dream was revived. I had met Bart and Dick at a meeting of the American Astronomical Society in 1954 in Michigan. I guess they knew something of my papers, and as I remember, I gave a paper there.[6] The possibility of a scholarship did not solve the problem of how to support myself. Carl proposed (literally) a solution. He would apply for a job at the Air Force Cambridge Research Laboratory, where he could continue his work, background research on sound to improve sonar performance, while I entered graduate school. It was too good to be true.

In August of 1955 we were married and the three of us moved to Cambridge, Massachusetts. We found a duplex apartment in an old building at Whittier and Walden Streets (no less) that lay less than a mile from Harvard College Observatory. It was quite spacious with a separate dining room and three bedrooms upstairs—all with acres of dark wood that gobbled up the light. The rather small living room had as its centerpiece a fireplace with a high-Victorian mantel complete with a hideous, mottled green marble facing. But then, there was a wide, handsome staircase that begged for either a grand entrance or a swift descent down the wide railing.

The Observatory, at 60 Garden Street, lies about half a mile away from Harvard Square (with the Coop, shops, and pubs) and Harvard Yard (with its stately buildings and old-world air). Its grounds, including a long drive up a small hill covered with trees, are large enough to create an air of real seclusion. Two of the three buildings were made of brick (covered with the requisite ivy), and the main one was graced by a double staircase leading to the main entrance. The third building was new and efficient, but quite without the character of the other two. It was on its lower floor, somewhat below street level, where I was to share an office with Mary Jane Stewart, a second-year student. Our office had one unique heavenly feature—a harp! It was Mary Jane's, but I heard her play it only once. Campbell Wade, also a second-year student, had the office next to ours, and two months later I gave an engagement party for Mary Jane and Cam.

Five of us entered that fall of 1955, all full of anticipation and hope. We chose our courses that first semester with the knowledge that early in January we would face our first general exams. There were three: one each on the subjects of astrophysics and galactic structure, and one on the "rest," including primarily solar system studies. Only when all three were passed could the student think of choosing a thesis topic. Also there were two language exams, fortunately limited to scientific writing. I took the French exam that fall, but put off the German as long as I could.

At 29, I was about five years older than my fellow students. Although I had family responsibilities that most of them didn't, I had worked in astronomy for seven years and knew what I wanted and something of how to get it. There were at the time four women students out of 15 or 20, a percentage higher than anywhere else. Women had been part of the scene at Harvard for a long time, but only as clerks, volunteers, and assistants. There were however several remarkable women who were able to do significant work on their own. Annie J. Cannon, hired in 1896, published the definitive catalog of stars and their spectral types. Henrietta Leavitt and Henrietta Swope in 1902, working with Harlow Shapley, discovered the period-luminosity relationship for Cepheid variable stars. Helen Sawyer Hogg went to Harvard Observatory to work with Cannon and Harlow Shapley, but since Harvard did not then give graduate degrees in science to women, she received her doctorate in astronomy from Radcliffe in 1931. (My own diploma carries the signatures of both the president of Radcliffe and of Harvard.)

But then came Cecilia Payne-Gaposchkin[7]. After her undergraduate work at Cambridge, England she had applied to come to Harvard for an advanced degree in astronomy, and the application was made in the name C. Payne, omitting the obviously feminine first name. Only on her arrival did the administration discover they had admitted a <u>woman</u>. She was now on the faculty, though not as full professor, despite her reputation as a first-class astronomer. I remember that she took me once to the faculty club for lunch, mostly, I think, for me to observe that we, as women, were not allowed to go in the front door but slipped in at a side entrance. On a later occasion I would find Dr. Gaposchkin a sensitive and honorable friend.

My first contact with her was in her course on variable stars. Not much of the subject matter remains with me, but I can never forget the lectures for her rich, imaginative use of the English language. And while I was still a student she was appointed a full professor of astronomy at Harvard University, the first such appointment for a woman. She, in characteristic fashion, shared her joy with the current women students, and her formal acceptance speech was unforgettable. As she stood at the podium, a large, imposing, slightly untidy figure, she said, "I find myself cast in the unlikely role of a thin wedge." Laughter filled the room.

That first semester I also studied with Dick Thomas who taught the Solar Chromosphere and Corona course. Dick was a remarkable man from whom I learned a lot during our lifelong friendship. One of the first things he said to the new students was, "Call me Dick. We'll soon be colleagues, so you might as well treat me like one." He reminded us that our fellow students in graduate school were different from those in college. They would be with us throughout our professional lives. Dick was a man altogether without pretension, and he had very little patience with anyone who was "too full of himself." His uncompromising honesty got him into trouble of which he was largely unaware. He was not an easy friend, but an absolutely loyal one.

As a scientist he was definitely ahead of his time, but unfortunately conveying his ideas in a lucid, comprehensible way was not his strong point. I found this out very soon when during the first week I was so bewildered that I raised my hand to say, "I am lost. I don't know what you are talking about." To my amazement he was delighted. All that a student or colleague needed to do was to ask for an explanation, and he would make a real effort to explain. He was not always successful, because his ideas often challenged the assumptions that underlay all studies of stellar atmospheres. The primary assumption of a sort of equilibrium in the gas allowed the computation of a host of properties of that gas. That this assumption was patently incorrect and led to a false impression of understanding was part of Dick's fundamental contribution. The other part lay in showing it was possible to use a nonequilibrium model (at the price of considerable mathematical complexity) to arrive at a truer picture.

Although the idea of working with Dick on his ground-breaking study of stellar atmospheres was tempting, I chose not to do so for several reasons. Real progress in observing the solar atmosphere was likely only after we could observe from above our atmosphere. This was 1956, when the prospect of making such observations was, to put it mildly, dim. In choosing a topic for a thesis a student is wise to beware of an open-ended project, one that depends on developments beyond her control. Thereby lies a long, frustrating time as a graduate student. In contrast, radio astronomers at Harvard were clearly poised to make significant progress. Dave Heeschen and Ed Lilley had just finished their theses on the study of interstellar hydrogen as an indicator of the structure of our galaxy. On the strength of their results Prof. Bart Bok had built a 60 foot radio telescope with a receiver for the 21 cm hydrogen radiation. He also gathered a group of eager, excited students. Who wouldn't be inspired by a man who said, "Think what you have. Here is the most powerful instrument in the world for studying an exciting new field, and it is all yours!"

With it we could even look beyond our own galaxy to study other galactic systems! Dave Heeschen had observed two relatively nearby galaxies, M51 and M81. (They have these numbers because they are objects number 51 and 81 in Messier's catalog of "fuzzy" objects. It's a bit like calling all objects emitting radio radiation "radio sources.") He found that in both cases the 21 cm radiation extends far beyond the optical limits of the system, suggesting that each is embedded in a great cloud of hydrogen. A quotation from an article Dave Heeschen and I wrote when I was a graduate student in 1957 expresses the lure of observations of interstellar hydrogen in <u>other</u> galaxies:

> *"21 cm line observations of an extragalactic system can yield directly the distance of the system, and the distribution, internal motions, and total mass of neutral hydrogen within the system. Indirectly, comparison of optical and radio data should yield information about the nature and evolution of galaxies and clusters of galaxies."*[8]

In other words, "the sky's the limit." It was an exciting prospect and we all knew it.

Much of this lay in the future, but I was able to choose for my thesis a study of the nearby galaxy M33.[9] The galaxy has a classic spiral structure, outlined by its brightest stars. It is in our local group of galaxies, and has been extensively studied. Because the interstellar gas associated with the system extends far beyond its optical image, the resolution of our antenna (53 arc minutes, almost twice the observed size of the moon) was adequate for the study. In 1962 with the addition of a much more sensitive receiver I was able to extend and improve my original observations.[10] They led to the velocity of the system with respect to us, the mass of neutral hydrogen in the galaxy, and its total mass. We knew that studies like this could make substantial contributions to our knowledge of galaxies beyond our own.

The antenna, a dish 60 feet in diameter, was mounted at Agassiz Station, Harvard's astronomical observing site about a 45 minute drive from Cambridge. It was a lovely, wooded area with several optical telescopes as well as a simple but comfortable house for observers. The radio telescope with its small building housing the controls and recording equipment lay quite separate from the other buildings and at a lower level than the others. The approach along the dirt road was a dramatic one, because the large, white dish appeared suddenly as you started down a steep hill—a view that always gave me a thrill.

I began my observations there in late September 1957. It was just at this time that Prof. Bok left Harvard to become director of the Mt. Stromlo Observatory in Australia. And then in early October things took an unexpected, dismaying twist. One afternoon in Cambridge I was asked to come to the director's office. I was surprised because student affairs were generally handled by the head of the astronomy department. I speculated that he might want to know something about my planned thesis topic. The events of the next half hour are etched in my memory so clearly that I can recall details of my surroundings after 45 years. When I came into the large room I was surprised to find several people already there. At the head of a long table sat the director, to his right the department head with his administrative assistant (a woman), to his left Prof. Thomas Gold, my thesis adviser, with a chair beside him for me. I was mystified. When

I was seated Dr. Gold said, "Nan, tell us about your thesis." With such an audience I happily described the results so far and my plans for completing the observations.

It was then that the director said, "Well, that's not actually what we called you here for." After a pause, "It has come to our attention that you are trying to break up the marriage of one of your fellow students." I am sure that my astonished, "What?" came out as a strangled squeak. I followed it with, "Who?" He told me and said, "He knows about this meeting. We told him that if he warned you about it, we would take that as evidence of the truth of the accusation." I must have said something like, "What are you talking about, and where did you get the idea?" The department head answered me by telling me that one of the other female students had voiced her suspicions to his depart-ment assistant and to my husband. (This account is hampered by my avoiding proper names.) It was at this point that I realized there was no point in my denying the absurd charges. My fear, of course, was that they would tell me to leave the Observatory, but I suddenly realized that they would not do that. Harvard treasures graduate students who are likely to succeed.

I will never know how I kept my head enough to ask simply, "What must I do to stay here?" They had that all figured out. I could continue my observations at Agassiz Station, but could not come to the Observatory except on Thursday afternoons to hear colloquia and use the library. If the price of my Ph.D. in astronomy included abiding by these humiliating requirements, so be it. I came away with the utmost contempt for the people who had done this to me. It meant a lot that there was one senior faculty member who had refused to be a part of it—Cecelia Payne-Gaposchkin. She shared my feelings.

On April 13, 1958 I took the final oral exam for my Ph.D. It was more grueling than normal because I was five months pregnant.

AIR FORCE CAMBRIDGE RESEARCH LABORATORY, 1958-1965

In the fall of 1958 with my doctorate (and new baby, Mary Nan) in hand, I, along with my fellow students, began to worry about where to find a job. For many years money for astronomical research had not been plentiful, but in October 1957, the Russians put up Sputnik, with a resulting change in the national attitude toward things astronomical. The National Science Foundation gave me a one-year fellowship at Harvard to examine 21 cm radiation from another nearby galaxy, M31, the Andromeda Nebula. My proposal was based on the greatly increased sensitivity expected from Harvard's new maser-based receiver. The receiver operated on the same principle as a laser, with either light (l) or microwave (m) amplification by stimulated emission reaction. Ours was a new attempt to use this technique and required immersing the front end in liquid helium, introducing a new complexity in logistics. Sadly, I discovered that the receiver would not be ready until well after my year was over. I gave up the fellowship and set about job hunting.

At the Air Force Cambridge Research Laboratory I found two jobs. One was with the new Space Track, charged with keeping track of the growing number of satellites. The satellite tracking plan involved setting up very wide angle (Schmidt) telescopes that would be used to record the presence of satellites and to carry out astronomical research as well. The idea was to locate the telescopes at observatories around the world where they could be managed by astronomers, and used as well for astronomical research. The plan seems quaint now, but no one foresaw the magnitude of the task. My second job was with the Astronomy Section that funded basic research at observatories around the world. After the new Air Force 85 foot antenna was completed I spent most of my time doing my own research.

The combined jobs made possible my first trip to Europe in 1960. I was to visit several observatories whose work we were funding and several others that we were considering as sites for the Space Track telescopes. I knew I could leave the children: by this time Mary was two years old, and fond of the woman ("Nursey Cook") who came to the house to care for both girls. In addition, Carl would enjoy the time with them. So I set off on ten days that could have been described as "It's Tuesday; it must be Belgium." Traveling under the auspices of the United States Air Force was a mixed blessing. (Something odd happened when I picked up my diplomatic passport: I had trouble signing across my picture. I hoped it wouldn't matter.) When I learned that on the journey I would have the rank of Colonel, I had visions of traveling in style. At Andrews Air Force Base, after some delay I boarded the military aircraft, and encountered reality. It was, of course, not a jet (in 1959), had no insulation in the walls of the cabin (making it both cold and incredibly noisy), and had what are known as "bucket seats." Crossing the Atlantic required a stop for refueling at Gander, Newfoundland. Various delays, that no one explained, kept us there for so long that it was actually a pleasure to board our frigid, rattling airplane. Next stop, Paris! Well, not quite. First, we landed in the Azores without a friendly captain to announce what we were doing there or tell us when we might leave. The military airport has got to be one of the worst in the world, with a waiting room that doubles as a bar for the locals (even at 6:00 in the morning) and that has only one restroom (with no hot water).

Next stop, Paris? Not quite. Next stop, Madrid! For some reason we could not land at Orly, France, and needed to spend the night at Torrejon, the airbase outside Madrid. It was far more civilized, and even included a good restaurant and the possibility of a ride into the city. However, after a good dinner and two glasses of wine my only thought was of a warm bed.

Then I realized that my friend, Jean-Claude Pecker was expecting me in Paris. In 1955 when I came to Harvard, Jean-Claude Pecker was there on a year-long fellowship with Dick Thomas. I remember giving a dinner party for him where I served a wine of dubious origin. Then I discovered his knowledge and appreciation of the best vintages of France. He was so utterly French: he got me out of the embarrassment with Gallic charm. Now I needed to contact Jean-Claude to tell him I had been delayed. After finding a telephone that would allow me to call off the base I had to deal first with a Spanish operator who eventually understood that I wanted to reach Paris and then with a French one who was somewhat less than helpful in doing so. At long last the telephone was answered but by a stranger who spoke no English. I figured out that any complicated message was out of the question, and therefore tried in my best Parisian-accented French, "Je suis Americaine"—hoping that would convey the fact that I was on my way. Alas, the woman did not understand. I was crushed. Only later did I find out that she was the cleaning woman who spoke only Spanish.

Finally however I did reach Paris where my friends gave me a fine dinner and a bewitching tour of the city. I then went on to Padua, Italy, where I was to be met by the Observatory's director (whose name I can't remember) and a visiting German astronomer, Karl Wurm. I walked into the large station and looked discreetly around, very discreetly this being Italy. Very soon I realized there was no one there to meet me, and avoiding thoughts of what might happen if no one came, I planted myself under the large station clock. After about half an hour panic was beginning to win out. After almost an hour of fielding curious glances I saw two middle-aged men striding across the room to me. Their explanations and apologies tumbled over one another. I think they spent the next few days making it up to me.

As I look at the map of the Italy I can see that they gave me a grand tour of northern Italy. My chief memories seem to be of food. It was here that I learned that an Italian meal often consists of antipasto, followed by pasta, followed not by dessert but by a main course. My discovery was a great source of amusement to my hosts. The final treat was an afternoon in Venice.

The Observatory is at Asiago, just north of Padua, where we talked of the possibilities of astronomical cooperation (of which I remember very little). I do remember a walk in the nearby countryside with Dr. Wurm, where for the first time I heard a real, live cuckoo. As I looked around he asked, "What's unusual about these trees?" When I couldn't answer he said, "They're all the same height. The forest was all cut down for firewood during the war." Memories of that time were clearly very much alive.

When I got back to the lab, I started my first research project, an investigation of the validity of the accepted model for our galaxy—ambitious and misguided, it turns out. Interstellar hydrogen observed at radio frequencies can be a powerful tool for studying our galaxy, but its distance can be deduced only indirectly, usually assuming a model of the galaxy. Another possibility for estimating its distance lies in connecting it with a feature whose distance can be found in a different way. I used published observational material to look at the interstellar neutral hydrogen in the direction of special groups of very young stars whose distance was known. Distances derived from the stars in the associations and those derived from the velocity of interstellar gas on the basis of the model were different, suggesting that our model of the galaxy needed revision.

This program illustrates the pitfalls in astronomical research. The results were published[11] in the Astrophysical Journal where all contributions are examined and passed by a referee (some-one familiar with the topic). After publication a colleague pointed out to me that my work was fundamentally flawed, because of a difference in the two kinds of observations. Apparently the optical observations of stellar velocities are based on a different zero point from that of the radio observations. When measuring the velocity of any distant object by observing its Doppler shift, one must decide how to allow for the velocity of the observer herself, due in part to the earth's motion around the Sun. Optical astronomers have long corrected for this motion and recorded the velocity of the object to the Sun. Radio astronomers have chosen to make a further refinement by correcting for the motion in the galaxy of a small group of stars that includes the Sun, the local standard of rest (LSR). I unfortunately overlooked the difference, making my challenge to the model of our galaxy simply wrong.

The experience reinforced my notion that I would have most success in observing rather than theorizing. Soon after I started at Space Track I found the opportunity to work out the best way to determine satellite positions on photographs. The method is very similar to the system we used for measuring variable stars from Nantucket. I also, as a distinctly junior author, published a paper in 1960 on the use of astronomical measurements for geodesy.[12] The senior author was Lt. Bruce Murray who went on to bigger things, including a key role in the first close-up photographs of Mars, and later as director of the Jet Propulsion Laboratory at Caltech. It's in this way that in the relatively small community of researchers at that time we came to know one another—never a bad idea to have friends in high places.

By 1962 there were about 15 satellites orbiting the earth, and the techniques for predicting their future locations were only slowly growing more reliable. I kept hearing, "We are on the brink of solving the problem." One mathematician said ruefully,

"Sometimes the brink can be very wide." On one occasion I was very glad to be only an innocent bystander. Someone decided that it would be a good idea to publish a list of known satellites and their positions. Not a good idea, it turns out. Among the satellites listed was one newly discovered and unidentified. Word came from what is known as "the highest level" that this was an American spy satellite that was supposed to be a secret! I had visions of an angry President Kennedy snapping at somebody, "Who did this?"

In 1962 Harvard allowed me, as a research associate, to use the 60 foot radio telescope on which I had done my thesis. I observed interstellar hydrogen in two other nearby galaxies, M101[13] and IC342[14], and set an upper limit to the amount in a third, NGC 5128[15]. In each case where it was detected, the gas extended well beyond the optical image and I could determine the mass of hydrogen and the total mass of the galaxy. Also, I saw in the observations the possibility of determining the distance of any galaxy based only on its mass of interstellar hydrogen compared to its total mass. The new method relied on the assumption that the percentage of hydrogen gas compared to total mass is about the same in similar galaxies. I must say that it was not until I began writing this story that I even remembered that I had published this result. I didn't remember because nobody seemed to notice it. My guess is that the astronomers who had been studying galaxies optically for a very long time failed to appreciate the contribution radio astronomers could make to their field. These were the first baby steps in our discovery of the power of radio astronomy.

In early 1963 the 84 foot radio telescope of the Air Force Cambridge Research Laboratory was completed. Since in the same year scientists at the Lincoln Laboratory of MIT had found the first evidence at radio wavelengths of another constituent of the interstellar gas, OH (the hydroxyl radical), we equipped the telescope to pursue the discovery. They had found the OH molecule was absorbing radiation at 18 cm from the direction of Cassiopeia A, the brightest radio source at this wavelength. In any project like this the first months are spent perfecting, testing, and coddling the usually unstable system. We, along with two other groups, were able to confirm and extend the observation of OH.[16]

The time is memorable for me, however, for reasons that have little to do with science. On the afternoon of Friday, November 22, 1963 we were planning our observations for the weekend when we heard the news of President Kennedy's assassination. We decided despite the shock to go on with them. As a result the weekend had a surreal quality. The receiver was housed within the large conical mount of the telescope where there were no windows, and only the presence of continuous reports over the radio kept us in touch with the real world.

But I had a closer touch with these real events. Just around this time I had been conferring with the producer of a television series called "Science All Stars," a show that included both young hopeful and established scientists. Taping was scheduled in New York for the following weekend. There I met Dr. Jerry Wiesner, Presidential Science Advisor, a distinguished scientist with a surprising sense of humor. I flew that Sunday morning on the Eastern Airlines shuttle from Boston to New York and was met by a car from the TV station. The atmosphere was not quite "red carpet," but close. When the taping was finished, the respectful treatment was over. How we got home was quite up to us. By then it was snowing and blowing on the streets of New York, and the airport was in turmoil. With dismay we saw long lines at the shuttle terminal both for flights to Washington and to Boston. Dr. Wiesner said, "I must get back to Washington," and after a pause, "I don't like to do this, but I will." With that he pulled out his magic White House card, and we were off. I protested (not very loudly) that he need not get me on the plane to Boston, to which he replied "Nonsense!" What fun to be "queen-for a day!"

We had dinner together before tackling the transportation problem, and I treasure our quiet conversation, because he told me of the scene in the White House just over a week before—on November 22nd. He and other members of the administration were meeting in the Cabinet Room when the Secretary of Defense was called out of the room. Dr. Wiesner said that on his return the look on his face made many guess that an atomic bomb had been dropped somewhere. No one guessed the truth.

Nan at Harvard. Photo courtesy of Doc Ewen.

LEXINGTON, MASSACHUSETTS, 1958-1965

In the summer of 1958, when Carl and I discovered that Mary Nan was due, we decided to do two things. First, I arranged for Carl to adopt Amy, so that all four of us would have the same last name. Second, we moved from the apartment in Cambridge to a house in nearby Lexington. It was a small, brick house on a quiet street with enough land for flower gardens. We also added two Siamese cats (Rigel and Vega) to the family.

Despite these acts of faith in the future of our marriage, at that time, after three years together, we were both feeling uncertain about it. Much changed, but writing this has led me to remember the early days. Carl filled our house with the sound of beautiful music through the most advanced hi-fi equipment, and taught me much about music in general. Two of his favorite compositions were Barber's "Adagio for Strings" and Berlioz' "Symphonie Fantastique," and hearing either brings back those days. Two of the many concerts we went to stand out in my memory. One was held at MIT in a relatively small concert hall with the Boston Symphony playing among other things the Berlioz Symphony. This particular Symphony is in part very, very loud with all the instruments, and especially the percussion, playing at once. Unfortunately our seats were in the front row, so that the sound was deafening, but fun. In the second we were also very close to the source of the music, but with happier results. It was a recital for solo cello held in the small hall of a Washington art museum, and again we were in the front row. The soloist played compositions by Kodaly, including one in which the composer called for the cellist to bang the instrument with the bow. A unique sound from ten feet away.

To be honest in this story I must make an effort to remember the good times, because so much bitterness followed. Also I must face the fact that some of it is my fault. Carl was more than generous in helping me to go to graduate school and in giving me the time I needed to work and to travel. I did not realize how damaging to him my enthusiasm and dedication to my work would be. It was a lot for me to ask. By the time I started working on my thesis we had fallen into the petty, wounding dialogue that poisons a marriage. Although Carl knew in advance of my summons to the director's office that dreadful day, he did not warn me (even though he didn't believe the accusation).

Amy was the glowing light in the gloom. She was a dear child with a definite mind of her own. When we were discussing possible names for the new arrival, she said, "I'm going to call her Mary. I don't care what you call her." She had a surprising talent for music, including (to the envy of her mother) perfect pitch. She began piano lessons when she was five, and could read notes before she could read words. I sat with her as she practiced, and those hours are among my most precious memories, along with a vision of her at piano recitals in a fluffy dress with her feet swinging high above the floor. We were all thrilled at the sound of her new piano—an old Mason-Hamlin concert grand with a meltingly beautiful middle range. The black lacquer had been removed to reveal five or six different kinds of wood, providing at each end of the keyboard perfect platforms for the two exotic cats.

Not long after we moved to Lexington I'd begun to have some strange and mildly troubling physical symptoms, one of the first being the difficulty in signing my name in my passport. Then there was something odd about my walking, a feeling of unsteadiness especially going down stairs. Also something strange happened to one of my eyes (I don't even remember which one) when I looked at a light. It was as if I were seeing an overexposed photograph. My policy usually is, if I ignore it, it will go away. But by late summer in 1960 I had to ask our family doctor for his advice. He did the things a doctor does when he doesn't know what the trouble is. After several weeks he suggested that I go to the hospital for a spinal tap—no big deal, just to settle things. Well, it was a big deal to me when I came out of the out-patient procedure with a crashing headache that persisted for ten whole weeks. From the way the doctor described it, the result was hardly worth it. "Nothing to worry about. There's really nothing you need to do except be careful."

About a year later, Amy and I were watching television while Carl was in the kitchen. The program was an episode of the Dr. Kildare series—the first of the disease-of-the-week genre. As usual, drama and tragedy dominated the hour. At the end I walked into the kitchen and was greeted by Carl with, "Well, now you can't avoid knowing what you have." That was how I learned I had multiple sclerosis. The doctor had told Carl and not me! I scheduled an appointment to tell him that he had put a shattering weapon in my husband's hands. (By the way, I received a bill for that appointment that I tore in tiny pieces.)

When I was able to think again I decided how to cope with this new factor in my life. For the first time I resolved to learn nothing (or as little as I could) about the details of the disease. The decision was based on the fact that the symptoms for an individual patient are entirely unpredictable. As that patient I could not know what to expect, and it was a better strategy to face a symptom when it appeared. As an example, my difficulty in signing my name (my first indication of trouble) did not extend to other uses of my hands, perhaps because writing your signature is probably a "hard-wired" process.

As it was with Amy, after Mary Nan was born, things were never the same again. She soon grew to be a sparkling toddler with abundant energy and frequent laughter. At ten months she began running, eliminating altogether the sedate business of walking. Her father was enchanted. As she grew older it was apparent that she was becoming the center of his life. It was quite clear to Amy and to me that Carl preferred Mary to either of us. That made me the disciplinarian—not an easy task with a willful little girl who could always turn to her father for support. One evening at dinner Mary picked up a sharp knife. She paid no attention to my "Put it down, Mary," or to my reaching for it. As a result my finger was cut to the nerve.

In her earliest years her spirits were dampened only by frequent urinary tract infections. Finally when she was about five years old she needed an operation to correct the problem. It was a new procedure with some risk, so that it was with a measure of dread that we left her at the hospital the night before. The next morning as we waited for word from the surgeon, I attacked the weeds in my flower garden (no doubt pulling up some flowers in my zeal). After a very long time Carl came to the door with relief on his face so that I knew all was well. In her hospital crib she looked very small and very wan and, of course, very precious. It was hard to leave her there.

Carl and I had come in separate cars, and I expected him to have reached home before me. When I came in and was greeted only by the cats—no Carl and no Amy, I was puzzled, then worried. At that moment Amy's friend from across the street came to the door with the news that Carl had taken Amy to the doctor. Amy had fallen out of their apple tree and broken her leg. Ah, the joys of motherhood!

Amy was very upset at the possibility that her trip to Europe, planned for the summer, might be canceled. She was to go to visit her Aunt Kit, her father's half-sister, who was living just north of Paris. Amy and I were to meet in Switzerland and spend a week there before I went off to a meeting of the International Astronomical Union in Hamburg and she went back to Paris. The doctor pronounced that if the cast were off her leg (in about six weeks) and she was managing with one crutch, she could go—and we did. He warned that we must arrange for her to go on with strengthening exercises, increasing the weight by one-half pound every day or so. Arranging that required some planning, including the use of a sandbag. It seemed a daunting task, but we failed to predict how a pretty little girl on crutches would be showered with offers of help.

As the time came to go home I realized that I was not looking forward to it, that there was a black cloud waiting for me. I didn't know how, but I knew I must end my marriage. With MS, I did not know how long I would be able to live an active life, but I knew I wanted to make the most of it. Aside from my own unhappiness, there was Mary to consider, especially after I discovered a new pattern. When she cried out in the night (which was often) Carl went to her bed, where he spent the rest of the night. I didn't think there was anything sinister about it, but no daughter should feel she is taking her mother's place. That had to end.

The next few months were a nightmare that I can't re-create now because I know how it all turned out. I knew it would not be easy. Carl put up every obstacle he could to my leaving with the girls, and said he would cooperate only if I left Mary with him. Everything seemed uncertain—everything. By early December 1964 the atmosphere at home was oppressive. The whole situation was making me more nervous, and less able to eat and sleep. A friend, Dick Thomas (then at the University of Arizona) suggested that I write what I had done in astronomy in the past 20 years and what I hoped to do in the next 20. He insisted that I send the results to him as I wrote them, because otherwise I might not follow through. It was a godsend, and incidentally led years later to a published paper.[17]

I had to make a living, and I hoped at the same time to find a job in which I could devote more time to research. Friends are vital to such job hunting, and fortunately I had many. One in particular was Doc Ewen (the discoverer of the 21 cm line radiation) who, in addition to knowing everybody working in radio astronomy, was a friend I could talk to freely. After hearing my tale, he said, "Berkeley is the place for you. I'll call Harold Weaver tomorrow." Harold was the director of the Radio Astronomy Laboratory at Berkeley, someone I knew and liked. Not too long ago I had gone to his christening celebration for the new 84 foot radio telescope at Hat Creek, California. After Doc had prepared the way, I called Berkeley myself. I was certainly not prepared for the news the university operator gave me: "I'm sorry ma'am, but the Berkeley campus is on strike, and I cannot put your call through." My anxiety about the job made my reply less than courteous!

About a week later Harold Weaver called and said, "We'd be glad to have you in the Lab. The position will be open in March, and I hope you can be here then." My relief robbed me of my voice.

At that moment I realized all the things I needed to do. I needed cash for the move itself, for a car, and for all sorts of real and imagined contingencies. First (little as I wanted to do it) I stopped depositing my paycheck in our joint account, and prepared to cash in my retirement fund. My spirits were lifted when I chose the new car I would have delivered to Berkeley—a Ford Fairlane convertible, white with red leather seats. I wanted very much to move into a house rather than a motel so that the girls would feel at home, at least a little. I asked the administrative assistant of the Radio Astronomy Lab to find a house for me to rent. She agreed to try, but hesitated to make a decision for me. Finally she wrote saying, "I have found a house, but I'm not sure about it. It does have a fireplace and a view of the Golden Gate Bridge." My reply, "Sold!"

When Carl saw that I really intended to do this no matter what, and that the whole experience was wearing me down physically, he decided to help make the change easier. When the time drew near I told the girls as much as I could. For one thing I told them that they would be spending their summers with their father. We will probably all remember my reading Alice in Wonderland to them in the final days. During the same time a song ran incessantly through my head, *"Somewhere Over the Rainbow."*

1965-1977

BERKELEY - ARRIVAL, 1965

On March 3rd 1965, at 39 years old, with Amy at 13, and Mary at 6, I arrived in Berkeley to begin a new life. It is a date I celebrate each year.

We landed in San Francisco on a very foggy afternoon. Cecile Weaver, wife of the director of the Radio Astronomy Lab (known hereafter as RAL), met us at the airport with as warm a welcome as I could imagine. She drove us over the Bay Bridge and up into the Berkeley Hills, to stop in front of a small house on a tree-lined street called Scenic Avenue. Whether the street would live up to its name we could not know because the fog enclosed us in a small white world. Within that world we could see the bright pink blossoms of cherry trees along the road and the dark green, feathery redwoods everywhere.

The house was, like many in the Berkeley Hills, a two-storey, dark brown-shingled bungalow. Lying in front of the heavy green door was a bouquet of red roses, a splendid housewarming gift from Dick Thomas, my former professor and friend. As I looked around I realized how much the house had been prepared for us. I had scarcely thought of the problem of furniture, but here were chairs and tables obviously borrowed from the gardens and garages of my new colleagues. Somehow this brought such a flood of relief and gratitude for the warm welcome that I could scarcely speak.

As soon as Cecile had gone all three of us crept gratefully into bed—long before sunset. Sometime during the night I awoke and went out on my small balcony. It was dark; the fog had cleared, and a carpet of twinkling, colored lights stretched below me until it reached the Bay. Beyond the Bay in the distance were the lights of the Golden Gate Bridge! It was an unforgettable moment. Quite literally. I am not one for omens, but it was hard not to see this as a splendid new beginning. (Little did I know). And there was more. In the morning I could see among the trees in our steep back yard three California bluebirds, a variety I had never seen before. Perhaps it really was *"Over the Rainbow."*

The next day did nothing to tarnish the illusion. After the three of us had explored our new domain, we set out to find Amy's new junior high school that lay in the "flats," about a mile down the hill. We found it and enrolled her and then set out for home. It was all uphill. Climbing that was more than I could do, partly because I was just getting over the flu, and I went in search of a taxi. We found a telephone in a gas station, where we must have been a pitiful sight, because the attendant said, "Forget about the taxi. I'll take you up the hill in my truck." Just after we got home Maggie, who had found our house for us, came to take me to the campus. I remember little of the introductions and tour because it all became so familiar.

I had only been home a little while when there was a knock at the door. It was our landlord who apologized for disturbing us, but said there was something wrong with one of the roll-up blinds on the porch. His name was Garret Conklin. I went out with him to look at it, grateful for such a conscientious landlord. As we talked a little, my impression was of someone gentle and kind as well. When he had finished and turned to me, I noticed there was some dust on his jacket and reached up to brush it off. Rather a trivial detail to remember? Perhaps; but he never let me forget it.

BERKELEY - FIRST DAYS, 1965

I began finding my way to the supermarket, the bank, and the best places to buy furnishings for the house we had all come to like very much. In about a month my spirits soared as I drove out of the dealership in my white convertible with red leather seats—an extravagance, but well worth it. Amy was doing fine, but the time was very hard for Mary, not surprising since I had taken her away from her father, the center of her life. She hated her school and everybody in it, and twice ran away, although fortunately not very far. Her misery made me question my decision to leave Lexington, and made me worry about her whenever she was out of sight. I'm afraid I depended too much on 13-year-old Amy for reassurance and help in dealing with her sister. Both girls paid in some way for my actions, but there seemed no other choice.

But we had the whole Bay Area to explore. On one of the first sunny weekends Cecile drove us on the popular "trip around the bridges." We began in Berkeley driving North to the Richmond Bridge, one of the earth's ugliest bridges, but with a view south across the Bay that redeems it. And then as we drove across Marin County to turn south toward San Francisco, I sensed that Cecile had a surprise in store. We could see the ocean ahead of us as we twisted through the gentle hills and made one final curving turn to come suddenly upon a magnificent sight. There is really no way to describe it in words because the experience depends on absorbing all the sights and sounds and smells at once. It was, of course, the Golden Gate. The glory of the Gate itself, surely one of the world's most beautiful places, is enhanced by (arguably) the world's most beautiful bridge. Coming upon it suddenly is a splendid experience. As we crossed the bridge itself I felt the power of the Pacific Ocean to the west tamed by the Gate into the incomparable San Francisco Bay. At the same time the brilliant red girders and cables of the bridge flashing by made me feel safe within one of man's greatest structures.

The house at 1400 Scenic was less than a mile from the campus. I drove down Euclid Avenue, turned in at the North gate to the famous campus, and found Campbell Hall where I was to work. On the top floor I found my small corner, soon to be a proper office, surrounded by men (no other women) working both in the radio astronomy laboratory and in the astronomy department of the University. I was delighted to find that the two groups worked so closely together, because in many quarters radio astronomers were considered a breed apart. It was wonderful place to work with a wide variety of programs and with frequent lively discussions about all of them. The only real difference between the groups lay in funding, the money for paying radio astronomers coming from the National Science Foundation annual grants, and that for the teaching faculty coming from the University. I as an associate radio astronomer got the same salary as an associate professor, but because of the annual nature of our grants we did not have tenure. On the other hand we had no teaching duties.

Perhaps the greatest benefit of having the astronomy department near us was the presence of graduate students—a talented, dedicated bunch. On my first day I met the young man who was to be my favorite of them all—Miller Goss. He was the sort of student teachers dream of; one needed only to stand back and watch him grow. (We have remained friends all these years, and he recently retired as director of the National Radio Astronomy Observatory's Very Large Array and the Very Long Baseline Array.)

Of vital importance, of course, was Harold Weaver, who was not only director of the lab but also professor in the department. He and his wife became close personal friends, and my view of his contribution to my professional life is probably best expressed by an acknowledgment I wrote much, much later. "Harold Weaver has contributed both by sharing his insight and by maintaining a stubborn refusal to be convinced on too little evidence. I am grateful for both."

In the astronomy department there were about eight astronomers at that time, and in the laboratory there were four. They were all among the best in the country, and I was sure I could learn from every one. The support staff for radio astronomy included observers who lived near the Hat Creek Observatory site, east of Redding in Northern California, and two computer programmers in Berkeley. They were all vital to the operation. At the time much of the programming for data reduction was done by astronomers themselves, but Harold thought it better to assign the job to specialists. (In 1965 there were no general computer programs to buy at any price.) I was grateful that I did not have to cope with the cumbersome data handling that required punching countless cards and carrying them in boxes across the street to the mathematics building where the lower floor housed a large main-frame computer. To say nothing of devising the complicated programs to do the job.

I had one more tour to make before I could settle down to work. I wanted to go to the site of the radio astronomy observatory in Hat Creek, several hundred miles northeast of Berkeley. Someone suggested that we might enjoy driving north along the coast and through the great redwood forests. The roads were not the best, but after all we were not in a hurry. And it's a good thing we weren't because in the woods there were logging trucks carrying great piles of tree-trunks held precariously by inadequate chains—or so it seemed from behind one of them. Passing one on the narrow roads was not an option, so we crept along behind the slow-moving giants. The trees were wonderful but apparently endless. At long last we reached the road going east that would take us to Hat Creek, a fine California freeway. Unfortunately I had turned the wrong way, and by the time I was on the right road my weariness and frustration (and that of two little girls) took over. Only when I saw a flashing light behind me did I realize that I was flying along the road! My introduction to the California highway patrol was amazingly pleasant. The young, handsome officer was very kind and very polite while he gave me an expensive speeding ticket.

We were greeted at the Observatory by Warren Taylor, the resident chief of the site, with what I came to know as his remarkable blend of Texas gallantry to a lady and real respect to a scientist. Because of our haggard appearance he led us right away to the house reserved for visiting observers and their families. It was a charming California ranch house, one storey with wood paneling, large rough stone fireplace, and all the modern conveniences. It was one of four houses set among the trees and winding roads of the Observatory grounds. Of the others, one was for the Taylor family, one for the caretakers of the site, and one served as a dormitory for astronomers coming to the site alone. Altogether the buildings graced the land and provided a quiet, beautiful setting for scientists away from home.

Early the next morning while Amy and Mary explored the woods I drove down to the flat plain where the 85 foot radio telescope stood. From there I could see both Mount Lassen and Mount Shasta in the distance. A few years earlier I had come here for the dedication of the new telescope[18] and the celebration included a fried chicken picnic on the mound of lava left by a long ago eruption of Lassen. In a splendid photograph Ansel Adams captured the contrast between the precise, white, modern antenna and the black, rough, ancient rocks. At the foot of the antenna was a small white building housing the controls that moved the antenna and the equipment that recorded the data. The telescope was pointed to an object, which was followed as it moved across the sky, providing an extended time to observe it. The longer one recorded the radiation the better, because nearly all the objects of interest were faint. The radio radiation struck the big dish and was focused at the feed, a point far out in front of the dish where it was collected, amplified, and transmitted to equipment inside the building. When it was necessary to maintain or modify things at the feed someone needed to ride up on the "cherry-picker" to reach it—not quite a spacewalk, but close enough for me. The dish that collected the radiation was so large because both the sensitivity and the resolution of the telescope depended on its size.

The equipment inside the building was devoted to improving the signal/noise ratio of the radiation, to integrating it over time, to filtering it, and finally to recording it. All this "massaging" the data is necessary not only because the radiation is weak, but also because it is indistinguishable from the noise generated by the equipment. If you could hear what is recorded it would all sound like static. We can detect the presence of an object emitting radio waves only by observing an increase in the noise-level in the direction of the object compared to regions nearby or by an increase at specific frequencies compared to the background. Once an object is detected its data must be reliably and efficiently recorded. When I walked into the control room that day, I could hear the machine punching cards that were to be sent to Berkeley for analysis. (Within several years it was replaced by a quiet tape-recorder.)

Incidentally, signals generated from "intelligent life" elsewhere would be distinguished from all other radio radiation in that they would be coherent, that is, like a tone rather than like noise. Despite the fact that discovering such signals would be enormously exciting, I continue to feel that there are so many unknowns that the odds against such a discovery are too high. First, one has to choose the direction in which to look, at a star that is not too far away and that is enough like the sun to have a planet that could support life. Next we have to choose the frequency at which to look (something of a guessing game). And last, we must be looking at a planet at the precise geologic time when an intelligent civilization would have progressed technologically beyond us, but not so far that they would be likely to ignore us as irrelevant. We may be lucky one day, but I was not going to play that game with my career.

To bring about a major installation like this one requires the skill and effort of many people, all with extraordinary determination and patience. To begin with, someone must have a vision of how this radio telescope can be used to contribute in a major way to progress in science. Here that person was Harold Weaver. First he had to convince the University to provide the land, permanent buildings, and maintenance for the whole place. That cannot have been easy, but was probably not so difficult as persuading the National Science Foundation to provide the money for constructing the telescope, equipping it with the best electronic systems, and bringing astronomers to use it. Once the antenna was built the next step was to design and manufacture the electronic equipment that would provide the most sensitive and stable system possible for detecting and recording the astronomical data. It was David Williams (both astronomer and electrical engineer) and Tap Lum who set the standards and oversaw the manufacture of it all. (David is British and enjoys his cup of tea, but would never make tea at Hat Creek because he said the high altitude (all of 3421 feet) made the water boil at too low a temperature. All our teasing had no effect.)

Finally Harold and David had to find the large support staff that would make the system work and keep working. Since radio radiation at the wavelength we were using is unaffected either by daylight or by bad weather, they needed to train observers to help carry out the astronomical programs and technicians to keep the sophisticated and delicate electronics humming. I was lucky enough to come to California when the whole Radio Astronomy Laboratory was established, and I needed only to contribute research plans that would help make all this effort worthwhile.

Nan in the control room at Berkeley's Hat Creek Observatory, 1969.

BERKELEY UNREST, 1965-1968

During the time of our thrilling OH discoveries (and as I explain shortly, they were thrilling to all of us), much was brewing on the Berkeley campus. I have forgotten if I ever knew the reasons for the first student-University confrontations, but I was greeted with their effect. When I had called Harold Weaver in December 1964 about the possibility of the job and was told the university was on strike, my reaction, colored by my anxiety at the time, was "What? It can't be. It's a university." At the time I phoned it was the "free speech movement," but later became the "People's Park issue," and then the Vietnam war and finally the bombing of Cambodia. Near the beginning of the escalating unrest I discovered something important about Garret, my landlord, who was becoming a good friend.

One sunny spring day we were walking along a major path through the campus to reach a grassy spot for a picnic when we came upon a group of about 30 people. They were lined up across the path at Sather Gate, the main entrance to the campus, not actually a gate but a decorative metal arch. The "rules-of-engagement" between students and administration allowed for demonstrations so long as they did not block access for anyone. Confronting the line of demonstrators was a man of about graduate student age who was trying to pass through the gate and who in frustration was striking out with his umbrella. As we watched he was thrown down on the brick walkway by a very large man who began beating him. There were several other people who like us were approaching the gate, but it was Garret who went to his rescue. The large man (who seems to grow larger in my memory with every passing year) had his back to Garret but whirled around when he felt Garret's touch on his shoulder and hit him in the face with a clenched fist.

In what appeared to be slow motion Garret fell on the bricks, protecting himself by curling up like a sow-bug. That, by the way, was my vision at the time. As soon as I could see that he was not seriously hurt, I attacked the man myself by pounding on his back with my fists in a fury that surprised me. Fortunately for me, he was too occupied to notice, although that made me even madder. At that moment he ran away because policemen were arriving to help. One tended to Garret and hurried him off to the clinic to be examined while another asked me to describe the assailant. For ever after I have sympathized with witnesses who struggle to identify criminals. All I got out was "he was very big and wearing a blue ski jacket," not much help to authorities. As the rioting grew more serious there were many more security people around the campus who caused a good deal of resentment, but I remained grateful for their presence.

In this incident I learned not only about Garret but also about myself. I had no idea that I was capable of such violence, no matter what the cause. Also as I thought about it, my reaction surprised me in that instead of comforting the "fallen hero" I attacked the villain. My feelings for Garret were clearly deeper than I had suspected. It is difficult now to remember what I saw then in this man who would become the center of my life. I know that his gentle, rather protective, manner was just what I needed. The protection apparently extended to anyone in need of it, even a stranger. I came to know that he lived his life based on his own independent view of the world with apparently no concession to the opinion of others. (I found it was possible to modify his outlook but never by direct confrontation.) Garret was totally honest, absolutely without pretense, and often unpredictable.

OH, 1965-1968

Throughout my professional career there was always a question of whether I was an astronomer who happened to be a woman or woman who happened to be an astronomer. Among my scientific colleagues I was always treated as the former, with all the opportunities for pursuing a project of my choosing that I needed: observing time, and help from the support staff to bring my findings to publication. Less tangible but at least as important was the encouragement and interest of astronomers who viewed me as their equal. For example, two suggestions I made at Berkeley were accepted with enthusiasm. One was the practice of having tea before regular Thursday colloquia (on the roof of the building in fine weather), and two, on a more serious note, a program of tutorials for all the graduate students that included astronomy department faculty members and radio astronomy research scientists as well. The students came to know the wide variety of personalities and programs available to them, and we became aware of the talents and interests of the students.

It was easy for me to begin work because both Harold Weaver and David Williams were also interested in the OH molecule in the interstellar gas. They had in fact confirmed[19] the original discovery[20], just as Doc Ewen and I had at AFCRL[21], and had prepared the telescope to search for the molecule all around the galaxy. For all three of us the gas that lies between the stars was the focus of our research.

Actually interstellar space would be called a vacuum on earth—in fact, we cannot create a vacuum so complete as this. But there is material there, however elusive. It was first discovered by noticing in the spectra of some stars evidence that some of the starlight was being absorbed by material lying between the star and us. The discovery had been made more than 100 years ago[22], but study of this interstellar medium took a real leap forward when it became possible to "see" radio wavelengths as well as light. In 1951 the primary constituent of the gas, neutral hydrogen, was detected throughout the galaxy because it emits radiation at radio wavelengths[23]. This was especially valuable because detection did not rely upon the clouds lying along the line of sight to a star. ("Cloud" is actually not a very good term for the denser regions in the interstellar gas, because they are neither fast-moving nor changeable.) In 1963 another constituent, the OH molecule, was discovered because it absorbs radiation from bright "radio sources"—the radio equivalent of the background stars. The molecule was much more difficult to work with because it is very much less abundant than the hydrogen atom.

In basic research one sometimes needs to throw caution to the winds (or almost) and take a chance. Here at Berkeley David Williams and Tap Lum, another talented engineer, took that chance by building a very sensitive receiver at 18 cm, the wavelength of the OH molecule, in the hope that it would yield important new information about our galaxy. Little did they know. The relatively complex structure of the OH molecule (compared to the simple hydrogen atom) made its study in the interstellar gas challenging. The spectrum of OH shows radiation at four distinct frequencies: 1667, 1665, 1612, and 1720 MHz, all at approximately 18 cm wavelength. (It is convenient to refer to radio radiation either by its wavelength (i.e. 18 cm or 21 cm) or its frequency (i.e. 1600 MHz or 1400 MHz). The relation between them is: wavelength times frequency equals the speed of light, or $\lambda v = c$).

The 1667 "line" observed in the laboratory is about twice as intense as that at 1665, and about nine times that at 1612 and at 1720. Naturally searches for OH were made at the strongest frequency, 1667 MHz. However, OH was found in absorption only in the direction of the brightest sources. And to the dismay of those who hoped OH could become a tool like neutral hydrogen for studying the interstellar gas no <u>emission</u> from the molecule was found in searches around the galaxy. Despite the less than encouraging early results the staff at Berkeley continued perfecting the new 100-channel receiver for further OH studies. The 100 channels divided the system bandwidth (200 KHz) into independent narrow-band (2 KHz) signals with the object of examining details of the spectrum.

Planning the observations took a couple of months, or until early summer. From my point of view that was a good thing because Amy and Mary were to spend each summer with their father in Massachusetts, leaving me without family responsibilities. That might have worked if we had not taken on a new family member, a beautiful, glowing-red Irish setter, named Sean. He was big and not very bright—but very resourceful. I had to leave him alone at home during the day, which led to some funny incidents. And some were not so funny. In desperation we took Sean for dog obedience training where he came out second in his class. There were only two dogs in the class. To allow him out into the backyard Miller Goss came and rigged a "dog door" in the basement door. Apparently, however, Sean spent some time inside where he figured out how to open the refrigerator door, to which my only solution was tying a rope around the refrigerator every time I went out. I resorted to that after the advice to place mousetraps around the refrigerator to frighten him resulted only in each of the human members of the household being startled by the **CLAP** of a mousetrap.

One may get the impression from reports of exploding stars and supernovae and various catastrophic events that the gas between the stars is about as dynamic as the gas in our atmosphere. Not so. One thing was certain: on the scale of our lifetime, observations could be repeated and checked with every expectation that they would be the same year after year.

Beginning a new research project is triggered by different developments. Sometimes new and powerful equipment appears, suggesting that looking again at objects already studied may yield a clearer picture. Sometimes looking at a large number of similar objects—a sort of survey—yields more than statistical information. There are surprises and new insights. And occasionally one simply stumbles on a discovery. I made one in 1965.

In planning the research it is wise to be aware of the strengths and weaknesses of the equipment. For us the high resolution in frequency of our 100-channel receiver was a definite plus. In the laboratory the frequencies of the OH transitions are very accurately known, but in nature the velocity of each molecule changes that frequency: the Doppler effect. In a given cloud if a molecule is approaching us, the frequency is slightly higher and if it is receding, slightly lower. As a result the radiation is detected not only at precisely the central frequency, but at other frequencies nearby, depending on how fast the molecules in the cloud are moving. And now suppose that we observe not one cloud but two at once, with different velocities. The two clouds are not likely to have the same velocity with respect to us which means that the central frequency of each one will be different— not by much, but quite measurable. With our system it was quite likely that we would see two clouds at once or even more, because of the size of the antenna, 84 feet. That size determines how much of the sky we see at once; here it was half a degree, or about the diameter of the full moon. (One would like to have as high resolution as possible so as to distinguish between one object and another, but that requires either a very large antenna or development of a different technique.)

By June 1965 we were ready to begin our search for OH else-where, by looking for absorption in front of the fainter, not yet observed radio sources. We knew that the program would take a long time because the signals were not strong, and we would therefore have to spend many hours observing each source. We needed to divide the duties in this extended observational program. Harold planned the order of observations and monitored their quality; David and Tap kept close watch of the instrumental performance both in Berkeley and at Hat Creek; and I collected and organized the data to determine when we needed more observing time on a source. Of course we had daily and sometimes hourly conferences.

In due course we reached the source, designated W49. (This time the number comes from Gart Westerhout's list of radio sources found using the radio telescope at Dwingeloo in the Netherlands.) In its direction only obscuring dust clouds are observed optically, but behind them lies a large nebula similar to the Orion Nebula but much farther away and much more massive. Our first observations of W49 at 1667 MHz provided the greatest surprise since the discovery of OH. The line did not appear in absorption of the background radiation, but in emission, and its intensity was 100 times the upper limit set in searches elsewhere in the galaxy!

It really didn't make sense. OH had not been observed in emis-sion anywhere else in the galaxy, so why here in the direction of a background radio source. Absorption of the background yes, but emission? Since the 1667 was so strong, we looked also at 1665, expecting the emission to be about half as strong. It was in fact much stronger! It was obvious that we should stop assuming anything about OH in the interstellar gas.

So, we set out to search for OH in a variety of sources with no assumptions about the nature of the radiation. In setting up a list of likely sources I went for advice to Rudolph Minkowski[24], who was a senior advisor in the Lab. Rudolph was a valued (and loved) member of the staff. He was a joy to have in the group because of his wide experience, his wisdom, and his gentleness. Fortunately his office was just down the hall. Rudolph was often a member of the group of us who had lunch together in the student union. One day I ordered a glass of iced coffee, and as I poured cream into the dark brown liquid, making an intricate, swirling pattern he said, "That's what the interstellar medium really looks like." Then as I stirred the coffee to a uniform tan, "And that's how we see it." I kept the memory fresh in my mind whenever I was tempted to assume a simple, predictable model of the gas.

Dr. Minkowski's last project at Mt. Palomar was to oversee the making of a great atlas of the sky, photographed with a powerful, wide-angle telescope. The Palomar Survey of the Northern Sky was intended to cover all the sky north of a certain limit, to provide a reference for all astronomers. I knew therefore that Rudolf had an unmatched knowledge of the sky, and also that he had in his office copies of all the original photographs. When I asked him for suggestions about where to look he was obviously delighted, and confessed that he had taken one photograph below the southern limit of the Atlas. It was not in the published catalog, but he had a copy, and pulled it out rather like a magician with a rabbit. On the photograph was a large, complex and beautiful nebula designated NGC 6334. "Try that one," Rudolph said. We were to be very glad we took his advice. NGC 6334 also showed very strong OH emission at 1665 MHz, but another surprise lay in store.

In our search of many sources we found six with anomalous OH emission, including W3 (now called W3-OH), W49, NGC 6334, W51, W75, and the Orion Nebula.[25] We, of course, needed to establish this bizarre discovery beyond doubt, and accumulated many hours of observations on each source. The program in the end extended over two years. One day in October 1965 I was looking at a new observation of NGC 6334 and happened to have on my desk at the same time an observation made in July. As I put the two diagrams side-by-side preparing to combine them, I stopped. "There must be something wrong—they don't look alike."

I checked everything I could think of to be sure these were indeed observations of the same objects made three months apart. Such a thing had never been seen before. Things had been puzzling in the interstellar medium, but conditions did <u>not</u> change in a matter of months. In fact, both this source and the one in Orion changed in <u>days</u>!

Naturally, no one believed me. The assumption was that something was wrong with the observations, such as a change in the receiving equipment that would look like a change in the source. Fortunately, there was a built-in calibration. Some features of the spectrum remained constant—only a few changed. Nevertheless, the variability of OH emission with time met with considerable skepticism.[26] One of our colleagues in another lab called to say "I'm sorry, Nan, but it <u>doesn't</u> vary." To which I replied with a snap, "That's because you haven't looked long enough!" It is rare enough that one stumbles on a discovery. It is even rarer that one can be so certain.

Theoreticians concluded from all the evidence that something very unlikely was going on. Apparently in a few, isolated instances we were observing the OH because of the presence in the interstellar gas of a maser, the radio equivalent of a laser.

NEW PROJECTS, 1966-1968

Our observations of OH emission in six gaseous nebulae took a long time to accumulate and longer to interpret. As is usually the case with a large project like this, we talked about the results at astronomical meetings, both formally and informally, long before we were ready to publish the whole story. The reaction of our colleagues was just what we had hoped, and we savored it with delight. The publication in The Astrophysical Journal Supplement that included 56 pages of tables, drawings, photographs, and theories, was submitted in August 1967, revised (on the advice of an anonymous referee) in October 1967, and finally saw the light of day in September 1968.[27] A long time from the first observations in May 1965.

My next project was quite different. I was asked by the editor of Reviews of Modern Physics to write an article on recent work on the interstellar gas.[28] Flattering, but I knew that my knowledge of theoretical studies was far from adequate. Fortunately Miller Goss joined me in writing the paper. I was particularly glad to write the long paper because I enjoyed trying to make my writing as lucid and graceful as possible within the restrictions of brief scientific communications, and here I would be able to stretch my literary wings. The last paragraph of the paper remains true 33 years later: "Our intention was to describe the progress that has been made in building up a detailed physical description of the interstellar medium. The outcome has been a picture full of uncertainties, but one that gives the impression that the discovery of a few vital pieces of the puzzle will clarify it all. The search for these pieces is likely to be a fascinating pursuit."

As I look at this quotation now (in 2005) I don't think I would say that what is required is "a few vital pieces." The situation is more "new discoveries" that may turn our current ideas upside down. Actually my own work on what I call a "very small cloud," discussed later on, challenges our ideas of the structure of that interstellar medium.

It was time to find a new research project using the equipment at hand. We were unlikely ever to stumble again upon the wealth of surprises of the OH observations. Also in 1967 the Berkeley 85 foot telescope was no longer one of the largest instruments in the world, but its very sensitive receivers could yield significant results. The receiver at 1600 MHz developed for the OH-radiation could also be used to study line emission from galactic nebulae, the very objects in which we had found OH. Nebulae like the Orion Nebula are great clouds, as the name implies, of ionized hydrogen. Unlike the neutral hydrogen disbursed throughout the galaxy this ionized gas forms discrete objects emitting both light and radio radiation.

I carried out a survey of 39 of these objects to study both the structure of the galaxy and the internal conditions in these nebulae using radio recombination lines.[29] These are the radio equivalent of the transitions of hydrogen that are prominent at optical wavelengths. Such a survey does not have the excitement of a new discovery, but contributes to the slow buildup of information of a statistical nature, and occasionally turns up a challenge to one of the assumptions usually made in studying these nebulae. A method for determining their temperature included the assumption that it was uniform throughout, but this survey showed that the assumption gave consistently too low a value of the temperature. In fact, the observations suggested that the temperature decreased from the center outwards. This is the sort of conclusion about which one could say, so what? The hope is that coming closer to the truth in a small way can contribute to a more comprehensive truth in the future.

GARRET, 1968

At the same time I was discovering that I had an extraordinary landlord. I learned that Garret had recently retired as assistant dean of the Episcopal theological seminary in Berkeley, a position that required managing the finances and the building programs of the school. As a member of the faculty he also taught classes in the Old Testament, and occasionally served as a substitute in local parishes. But for the house he owned our paths would never have crossed. Not long after we met he left the ministry because, he said, "I find that I'm reading the words of the service but not feeling their meaning. I could not go on doing that." However, he retained his faith in a personal God, a view I did not share, but one I certainly respected.

We did not talk much of serious things, at least not directly, and I discovered that I was having fun again. We began a time of enjoying San Francisco Bay. Garret owned a small fishing boat and took me out on it one sunny afternoon. I enjoyed exploring the glorious Bay until suddenly the engine stopped. For a long time he, or rather his head, disappeared into the bowels of the boat while I kept very still. I wasn't really worried, because Garret somehow gave the impression that he could fix anything, not by saying so, but simply by his quiet confidence. And apparently I did the right thing, because I did not flutter about or ask what was wrong or even figuratively wring my hands. (Or so he told me later.)

Garret introduced both my girls and me to the joy of sailboats that were both quieter and more interesting than what we all learned to call "stink-boats." There was never any question of who was the captain of our rented sailboat both because he knew how to sail and because we learned that he apparently could do anything. Mostly his self-assurance was not irritating but rather soothing—we all felt safe. There was, however, one area that did bother me, his ability to handle the unmanageable (by me) Irish setter, Sean. This was undoubtedly the most infuriating four-footed critter on the planet. One day I was making veal scallopini, a process that requires slicing the expensive meat into small strips and sprinkling them with flour before browning in butter. I was nearly ready to cook the veal when I heard a shriek from upstairs. I ran up to find both girls in my tiny dressing room laughing at what appeared to be a whole boxful of Kleenex tossed about the room, obviously the work of our now large dog. I was not amused, and I realized all of a sudden that he was nowhere to be seen. I virtually flew downstairs to find him licking his chops. It didn't help that when Garret came by that evening Sean clearly recognized the presence of his "master," and pretended that butter or (veal) wouldn't melt in his mouth.

Garret's self-assurance never seemed to strike anyone as arrogance, perhaps because at the same time he patently respected others almost without exception. In fact, he had real respect for anything alive, including spiders and horses and butterflies, and certainly standard poodles. He was a man who accepted my devotion to my profession, celebrated my successes (sometimes with a piece of jewelry) and distracted me from my failures. Of course, I had only hints of all this at first as we enjoyed the restaurants of Berkeley and San Francisco and drove about in his yellow vintage Porsche. One evening as we were returning from dinner in Sausalito crossing the Richmond Bridge I looked up at the light flashing on the web of girders over my head. At that moment I knew I could not let this man go—I wanted to spend the rest of my life with him. I have a notion that he had arrived at a similar conclusion, because as overwhelming proof of his commitment he traded in the Porsche for a VW station wagon. So on Jan 12, 1968 we were married.

We were so different, but it seemed the difference did not divide us but enriched each of our separate lives. Garret was 59 years old and I was 41. He had volunteered in early 1942 for the Army and served overseas in the OSS (the precursor of the CIA). The Army recognized his talent for languages, but instead of using his already fluent French, sent him to language school in Minnesota to learn Swedish. At first in London and then later in Paris he decoded messages that came from behind enemy lines in all the Scandinavian countries. During his time at the seminary he spent one semester studying in Uppsala, Sweden, and it was no doubt that experience that led to his studying for a master's degree in Swedish literature at 59. The subject is one I would never have known anything about on my own, and I learned from him mostly how gloomy it is.

During the same time he was doing volunteer work for the seminary and for a suicide hot line. (I know that the suicide prevention group had a special name for this service, but I can neither remember it, nor can I ask him.) Typical of his willingness to help was an incident that happened in downtown Berkeley. As I heard the story later, he saw a group of police officers and emergency workers outside the Wells Fargo Bank, all looking up at the roof of the building where a man was threatening to jump. He offered, I am sure in his quiet way, to go up to try to persuade the man to live. Not only did he succeed, but he kept in touch with the man long after. It was a skill with people, quite beyond my ken, that came from a profound sense of duty and a boundless well of compassion. I knew how lucky I was.

CAMPUS DRIVE, 1968-1969

We needed to find a place to live and searched for a house to rent in the Berkeley Hills. In January there weren't very many, but we had a stroke of luck, or so it seemed. On Campus Drive, a winding road that ended at the upper and undeveloped part of the Berkeley campus, there was a handsome house built by an architect for himself. It was, in fact, quite grand. I confess that the "grandness" appealed more to me than to Garret, who saw some of the difficulties with actually living in the house.

From the outside, the tall house seemed to tower over the road partly because the front door lay at least two stories above it. Plate glass dominated the façade and there was a winding outdoor staircase to the second floor. Just inside was a spectacular living room built on two levels with the beautiful fireplace two or three steps above the main seating area. Above was a second floor balcony with the bedrooms beyond. I remember the moment when we returned in the pouring rain from our honeymoon weekend at Carmel Highlands to find a splendid fire in the fireplace and Harold and Cecile with Amy and Mary to greet us.

The not-quite-so-grand master bedroom and bath lay just off the living room and the other bedrooms and kitchen were on the second floor. Since the house was built into the hillside, the door from the kitchen opened onto a wide wooden deck at ground level. It all was indeed grand, but it did not take many trips up the outside staircase to the kitchen with a load of groceries to cool my ardor for the "grand." And then there were the skylights, all leaky in a rain storm, and the pervasive, constant scent of eucalyptus trees that surrounded the house. As Garret said, "Those trees drop everything—leaves, bark, seeds, and especially sap, and their roots seek out any water, including in pipes leading to the house." Amy, now 16, complained bitterly about her job of keeping the kitchen floor clean with "Who would want an absolutely white kitchen floor?"

Since our lease ran for a year, all we could do was laugh at the house and ourselves. Our mansion almost redeemed itself as a magnificent background for Christmas, and was a beautiful place for our first year as a family.

We did have an escape at our A-frame cottage in the Sierras overlooking Donner Lake. It was a perfect weekend retreat in the heart of ski country in winter and on the lovely and historic Donner Lake for sailing in summer. There were a few permanent residents and even fewer tourists in the quiet town, just the sort of place we liked. Snowfall was measured not in inches but in feet, and transformed the surrounding woods into a magic place with almost tangible silence and air so clear and cold it was, really, like wine. It was here that Garret introduced the girls to cross-country skiing which, characteristically, he preferred to downhill. I tried the skis until I found that when I fell I could not get up again. I could, however, stay on my feet on snowshoes and found that I could keep up with the skiers because although they went faster downhill I went faster uphill. (Clearly, any interference with my balance caused by MS was not interfering with my snowshoe treks, perhaps because my "feet" were so big.) We went often to the hills just below Castle Peak at 7000 feet and came to know it rather well. We were therefore surprised one winter to find a large group of evergreens about two feet high. And then it dawned on us—we were seeing just the tops of tall trees, the rest buried under 12 feet of snow.

In the summer we sailed around the peaceful Lake in our little 12 foot sailboat, "Galaxy" (!) class, and tried our hand at planting a mountain garden. During the first years Amy and Mary enjoyed it all as much as we did but the time came, of course, when it was all "boring." It helped when we had guests, their classmates, graduate students, and visiting scientists. Also, Christmas was always fun with a large tree from our own land shining with decorations in the large window covering the whole front of the house. And then there was Sean, the Irish setter, who had mixed feelings about the snow, plunging through deep drifts, red hair flying, but spending hours pulling clumps of ice out of his fur. One Christmas vacation he had very good time indeed. We often did the major cooking for the week in Berkeley—pumpkin and mince pies, meatloaf, and sometimes the turkey. The refrigerator at Donner wouldn't hold all these goodies, but we had plenty of room in the snow pack to preserve them—except from our too clever dog. If I was ever tempted to leave him behind to freeze, it was then.

Garret

HIGH COURT, 1969-1977

In January 1969 our lease was up on the "grand" house, and we bought a much more suitable one in the Berkeley Hills. In fact, I think it is my favorite of all those we lived in. It was on High Court, a cul-de-sac less than a mile from my first Berkeley house and with a view even more spectacular. At ground level in the front was a two-car garage and above it the large windows forming the wall of the living room. In the typical "California Ranch" style the living-dining area and kitchen were all open to the view of the Bay and the Golden Gate Bridge. In the back and down three steps was a hall with three bedrooms and two baths, and, best of all, an enclosed patio that was my favorite spot.

That first spring I planted rose bushes, or more accurately put them in the holes 18 inches in diameter and 18 inches deep that Garret dug for me, complaining bitterly all the time. I had no pity and put in as many as I could: Peace with its gentle yellow and pink, Chrysler Imperial with its fragrant, deep red velvety blossoms, and JFK, whose clear white buds carry drops of bright red. He drew the line, however, at vines against the house. There was already a vine against the back fence, actually a pyracantha bush espaliered against it. It was a beautiful sight, especially when the abundance of small red berries appeared in the fall, attracting all the birds in the neighborhood for a feast. Well, actually, it was more like a binge, because they all flew about in what was obviously a roaring drunk.

During these first years all four of us worked at becoming a true family. The girls were in school, making new friends and absorbing the new California atmosphere. For Mary it was a very difficult transition both because she was so young, and because she missed her father so. It was a mixed blessing that each summer both Amy and Mary went back to Massachusetts to their father. Garret and I enjoyed the summers alone, but I was always a little afraid that Mary would never come back. I'm sure that for Garret it was hard to adjust to the three new "women" in his life, because each in her own way was an independent spirit. We all came to rely on his quiet strength and unwavering fairness. That is not to say that there was never any of the inevitable friction that comes with being a stepfather, but together we worked it out.

Speaking of disagreements, Garret and I set up what might be called "rules of engagement" for our infrequent disputes. First, the argument should be about what it seems to be about, and not a substitute for deeper conflict. Then, neither of us should bring up past wrongs, real or imagined, as weapons in the current fight. They were never really "fights," because neither of us ever spoke to wound the other. Never for a moment was our absolute commitment to one another in any doubt.

During the first summer Garret introduced me to sailing, and it was to be a source of fun for us both for many years. He was as skilled at it as he was at everything, or so it seemed. I learned in various rented boats about controlling a very small boat in a very large Bay, and in particular that it requires a lot of energy. Somehow I had imagined sitting back with my arm draping gracefully over the edge while the wind carried us silently along. After a few sharp commands from the "Captain" I knew better. I came to know the real joys of sailing: the quiet broken only by the slapping of water on the hull and the cracking of rigging as the wind picked up, the feeling of warm sun and crisp breezes, and of course the view of the Bay from the level of the water.

We decided to buy a boat of our own, the search for the right boat at the right price being almost as much fun as sailing it, and we finally found one we thought would be perfect: a 29 foot

English sloop motor-sailor. One of the things we liked best about our "Nan C" was the set of brilliant yellow sails, because they were unique on the Bay. She had sailed the English Channel and was therefore up to the challenge of the Bay open to the Pacific Ocean. Sometimes it was a real challenge. The wind and waves sweeping through the Golden Gate often gave the water a quite distinctive chop and the wind a treacherous variability. I especially remember one day when we were sailing near Angel Island, just inside the gate, when a sudden change in the wind sent us much closer than we intended to a buoy marking the channel. A large seal sleeping on the buoy in the warm sun was none too happy to be awakened from his siesta, and made that abundantly clear by the way he slid into the water. Through our laughter we were able to avoid a collision.

Two of Garret's sons served in Vietnam, one in the army and one in the Coast Guard. After many anxious months Garret Jr. was coming home and his Coast Guard Cutter, the USS Taney, was to dock in San Francisco Bay. We learned that the city was planning a royal welcome, complete with fireboats and their fountains of water. Well, we could do them one better! Early that Saturday morning while it was still quite foggy, we set sail in the "Nan C" for the Golden Gate. We sailed under the bridge, which is quite an adventure in itself, and out a little way into the Pacific. After an anxious wait we saw a ship in the distance. It rapidly drew nearer, but it was obviously not going to come very close to us, and we had hoped so much that Garry would know we had come. Suddenly from the ship came a rapidly flashing brilliant light! We, of course, had no idea of the content of the message, but the meaning was clear. Garry had recognized the yellow sails.

MAFFEI 1: ABOVE THE FOLD!, 1971

The title of this section might be "My 15 Minutes of Fame" or "Reward for Finding Nothing." It began in 1968 when Paolo Maffei, an Italian astronomer, found two strange objects on an infrared photograph of a region of sky known to be full of interstellar dust. It was suggested that the two irregular patches of infrared radiation might originate outside our galaxy and if so would have to be very large. The idea that the radiation was coming from another galaxy, its light being reddened by passing through the dust, caused quite a stir. The apparent size and brightness of the objects meant that they must lie near our own Milky Way. "Near" in astronomical terms.

Our Local Group of galaxies has long been known to include five great systems: the Milky Way, the Andromeda Nebula, the spiral galaxy M33 (my thesis topic) and two irregular systems known as the Magellanic Clouds (after the explorer Magellan). The addition of two more galaxies to the group could be significant. As quoted in the newspaper, Hy Spinrad, an astronomer on the staff at Berkeley said, "It is unfortunate that the galaxies are situated just where they happen to be, behind all that interstellar dust. But, as the Milky Way rotates, the galaxies will eventually swing into full view of earthlings. But it will be 100 million years before that happens." I'm sure, knowing him, that he would have said that with a smile.

Eventually astronomers all over the country, including from Berkeley and Caltech, tried in every way they could to study the new object. The paper describing the results[30], published in The Astrophysical Journal Letters, has eight authors, mostly an impressive array of astronomers. Jan. 11, 1971 must have been a very slow news day at the New York Times. They published an account of the research on the front page above the fold! It includes a photograph of three of the Berkeley astronomers standing on a stairway outside a small dome. I am pictured at the top! Also the United Press picked up the story with a picture of the same three astronomers that has a caption that identifies them as "team leaders."

It is lucky for me that the other authors of the paper, and particularly my Berkeley colleagues, were able to laugh with me. My "leading" contribution consisted of agreeing to point the Berkeley radio telescope at the objects to see if there was any detectable radio radiation. I didn't find any. I've expended far more energy on other projects without any "above the fold" publicity. The whole history of the two Maffei galaxies is fraught with irony that I only learned about much later.[31]

HIGH VELOCITY HI, 1969-1971

It was time that I embarked on a new astronomical project of my own. The major programs of the Radio Astronomy Laboratory during the late 60s and early 70s were large-scale surveys of the radio radiation from the interstellar gas. The object was to study the overall structure and dynamics of our galaxy. Our sun is part of a great system of stars that form a galaxy. A photograph of it from above would show a beautiful pattern of stars forming what are called spiral arms. A photograph from the side would show it to be a relatively thin disc.

What no photograph would show is the diffuse gas that lies between the stars, because it radiates not light but radio waves. The neutral hydrogen atoms that make up most of the interstellar gas radiate at a very precisely known frequency: 1420.4056 MHz. That is the frequency observed when the atoms are at rest with respect to the observer. However, when the gas is moving, its frequency is shifted by the Doppler effect. By measuring the amount of that shift we can tell whether the gas is approaching us or receding from us, and how fast. Therefore, observation of the hydrogen atoms in the interstellar gas can give us new information not only about the structure of the galaxy but also about the motions within it.

Two groups undertook to gather data throughout the galaxy to take advantage of this new tool. Carl Heiles and Harm Habing surveyed gas lying out of the plane[32], and Weaver and Williams covered the major component of the gas that lies within the flattened disk of the galaxy[33]. The two extensive programs covered the whole visible sky, but were both limited in that they cover gas only at relatively low velocities with respect to us. My work extended the coverage to high-velocity gas, that is, gas moving at a velocity higher than expected on the basis of models of the galaxy.[34] Isolated clouds of neutral hydrogen moving at high velocity had been found, (including some I had found myself) but I wanted to see if there was widely distributed gas moving at similar velocities. Altogether my program alone required a major commitment of time and resources. For example, my survey required about 2500 hours of observing, and that was only the beginning. Recording, organizing, and interpreting the mass of data required far longer.

The observations were made during several periods from May 1969 to August 1970. At each of the about 4750 positions on the sky the intensity of the hydrogen emission was recorded in 100 separate channels of the receiver, each representing a range of 2 km/sec in radial velocity. This mass of data was handled in a way that now seems "prehistoric." It was recorded at the Observatory on punched cards that were sent to the lab in Berkeley where they were fed into the main-frame computer that took up a large part of the basement of the mathematics building. The programs designed to calibrate and synthesize the data were also fed in on punched cards. (This entailed a lot of carrying boxes of cards.) Fortunately for me, these programs had to a great extent been worked out for the other hydrogen surveys at the lab. The final presentation of the data is in the form of contour maps of the sky showing the intensity of the emission at each radial velocity. The result was about as awkward as my description. It is done much more elegantly these days.

The information on those maps presented a real problem in seeing the galactic "woods" for the cloudy "trees." For a long time isolated clouds of hydrogen that had velocities far outside those predicted on the basis of the rotation of the galaxy had been observed. I wanted this survey to locate all of them throughout our observable northern sky. The one thing they all had in common was a negative velocity; that is, they all appeared to be approaching the sun. As I struggled to assimilate the information I was given very valuable advice by Dr. V. L. Ginzburg, an astrophysicist visiting from Moscow. Dr. Ginzburg (whom I never learned to call by his first name) was a very distinguished scientist and a cultured, articulate man as well. He always gave me the impression of listening very carefully, not only out of courtesy but also because he was always ready to learn something new. We were lucky enough to be able to invite him to dinner at our house where I laid out some of the maps on the table in our patio to show him. He looked up and said, "Forget the details. Look at the big picture." When I did so I found something new.

I focused on the highest velocity observed at each position, and found that as I moved from one position to another that velocity changed in a systematic way. What I was observing was not a collection of isolated clouds in the interstellar gas but evidence of widespread, low-level emission from hydrogen gas at high negative velocity throughout the galaxy. The process of finding the highest velocity was fraught with more troubles than you might guess. Our position near the outer edge of a galaxy that is rotating in a complex way (not like a wheel), our ignorance of the distance of the gas, and our inability to measure velocity across the line of sight, all mean that we can get nowhere in understanding the system without a theoretical model of the galaxy.

The model that I proposed to explain my observations of high-velocity neutral hydrogen is a simplified one but also one that seems to work. The idea is that the high-velocity gas lies at the periphery of our galaxy, outlines the outermost spiral arms, and forms a sort of shell around it. This gas has a rotational velocity appropriate to its distance from the galactic center, and in addition has a component of velocity directed toward the center with a magnitude of 125 km/sec. Because we lie within the shell all the material in it would appear to be approaching us. The most obvious characteristic of the observations that it explains is the overwhelming preponderance of negative velocities observed (indicating material approaching us). On the basis of the model I predicted the maximum velocity to be expected at each position. My predictions were confirmed within the uncertainty of the observations and the probable irregularity of the motions.

The observations are by their nature uncertain. My particular interest was in determining at each point in the sky the highest velocity at which any emission was detectable. This means, of course, that the results depended on detection of the weakest signals—those just above the zero level of the equipment. Radio astronomers in Australia attempted to confirm my results by looking at the part of the southern sky invisible from California. If they had asked me, I should have told them that the model predicts no high velocities in that direction. They did not find any.

Unfortunately, for a variety of reasons the observations have not been checked by other observers. Since the observations were made very great improvements in instrumentation have allowed detection of neutral hydrogen in many other galaxies, but no high velocity gas has been found. It just happens that a "shell" like the one I proposed would be virtually undetectable in galaxies that are face-on to us because the model predicts very little, and in galaxies that are edge-on because the high-velocity gas would be hopelessly confused with the other motions in the system.

Dr. Jan Oort (1900-1992), then one of the world's most distinguished astronomers, had proposed a theory for the formation of our galaxy in which material would still be joining the system. Under that theory most of the high-velocity gas we observe is part of the normal galactic material that has been given an extra inward push by the inflow of gas from outside our galaxy. The material flowing in is thought to be a remnant of the conditions that led to the formation of our galaxy (and all galaxies). In an informal meeting in September 1971 at the National Radio Astronomy Observatory in West Virginia, (so informal that for some of the sessions we sat on a grassy hillside) I was able to tell Dr. Oort about my results. Since they substantiated his predictions, he was delighted, but in a way suitable for a gentleman of the old school.

Without confirmation of the observational results, models and theories remain only that.

GARRET 2, 1969-1971

During the same time I was making other, more personal discoveries. I felt that I knew the important and basic things about my new husband, but I was learning about the life that had made him the man I knew. He was born in 1908, 17-1/2 years before me, so that he had lived in times I knew little of. His mother and father were divorced when he was very young, and afterwards he had no contact with his father. (What I am writing is, of course, my interpretation of what he told me, a sort of double hearsay.) When he was about seven or eight years old, his mother sent Garret to Canford Academy, an English boarding school. His memory of the school was distinctly unpleasant, particularly since he was always cold and often hungry because he hated macaroni and cheese, and tapioca pudding, two dishes never served in our house.

I found it surprising that Garret never criticized his mother for sending him there, although he did remember with some pain spending holidays at the school while other boys went home. I don't know when he came to the point of accepting that his mother needed some freedom, but I suspect it was well after the fact. On the other hand, he treasured the memory of the summers spent with her in Cap d'Ai on the French Riviera. Perhaps it was there he discovered the fun of learning a new language and learning how his considerable skill at it opened the doors of a new country. I am guessing, of course, but I suspect he set one of the patterns of his life during this time. He might have said, although he never did, "Waste no time being a 'victim,' but make the best of it and without a hint of whining."

Garret went to a public high school in New York City that he credited with awakening the intellectual curiosity that pervaded his life. The effect of his college (Swarthmore) was, by contrast, in his view minimal, perhaps because he simply had a good time partying. It should be remembered that I am relying on an educated guess, but he certainly learned to enjoy drinking beer somewhere. He graduated from college in about 1930. There were of course no jobs for a liberal arts graduate, so he took night courses in accounting, sharing an apartment with a friend. Henry and Garret became a formidable team at bridge, so formidable that they made enough money to live on. Incidentally, I never saw Garret play, perhaps because he could never look upon it as a game. One day much, much later he said something that gave me a shocking vision of how poor they were. When I commented upon his fondness for bananas, he said, "I used to eat a lot of them because they filled me up. Then I didn't feel so hungry."

Never one to lie down in the face of challenge, Garret hatched a scheme for gaining "experience," a vital commodity in job-hunting. He went to the owner of a shoe store in a poor part of the city with a proposal: he would work for three days without pay if the owner would teach him to sell shoes. Next stop, Neiman Marcus where they hired him! An echo in our life of this experience was Garret's dislike of shopping in general and absolute refusal to shop for shoes with me.

Living through the ordeal of the great Depression affected him in a much more serious way. In his mind there was always a possibility that our economic security would vanish. He never seemed to escape this emotional uncertainty. Since I had been a child during that time, our views about money were different, but the difference caused a minimum of friction no doubt because of the way he did spend money. He was a sucker for something beautiful (a fine wood carving), something uniquely useful (an ingenious tool), or especially something he knew would please me (an apartment in Paris).

HIGH COURT 2, 1969-1977

We took full advantage of living in the vibrant community that is the Bay Area. An evening out for us began with the drive across the Bay Bridge, a bridge that provides its own thrills, particularly when going toward the city. The sight of the black water and beyond it the magic tapestry of sparkling, colored lights is unforgettable, giving an air of festivity to any evening in San Francisco. And the food! We found many favorites: a small Creole restaurant with very spicy food, the Shadows just below Coit Tower with a splendid view, a Japanese restaurant where one left one's shoes at the door, and, of course, Fisherman's Wharf, which would be fun even without the sourdough bread and splendid seafood.

On a more cultural note, we tried a subscription to the San Francisco Repertory Theatre, but found the offerings too uneven for us both. (We agreed surprisingly often in our reactions to the plays.) We had more success with the San Francisco Symphony after I persuaded Garret to try. He knew very little of classical music, but after hearing a few of my choice records and a few concerts, he was hooked. He always preferred the sweeping, romantic, and loud orchestral pieces. That brings me to a very special concert. The San Francisco Symphony had recently hired Seiji Osawa as conductor and announced a concert that included the newly famous pianist, Vladimir Ashkenazy. He was to play a piece that was sure to please Garret, Rachmaninoff's Piano Concerto #3. The concert turned out to be that rare musical occasion that leaves the audience silent for a moment before its prolonged applause. Neither of us will ever forget it, and in fact when we listened to our own CD, we heard that performance again.

We stopped that evening as we often did after a "night on the town" at Brennan's, a large, mostly empty cafeteria-bar under the freeway in Berkeley. For us the attraction was their superb Irish coffee, complete with cold, heavy cream floating on top. As I remember sitting there in that somewhat bleak place, I can almost re-create the feeling of quiet happiness that surrounded us. On such excursions Garret always surrounded me with consideration and even gallantry—especially remarkable because he also showed a profound respect for my lively independence. In fact, there were times when he looked at me as if he could hardly believe that I was really there, a memory for a lifetime.

Nan in the Bodega house during construction, 1974.

BODEGA, 1971-1977

Fortunately my health interfered very little during this time. In fact, at the lab no one knew about the MS but my boss, and I nearly forgot it, except for the times when an extreme weariness overtook me. I found, however, that on our weekends at Donner Lake I was having more and more difficulty breathing, so we had to make a change. We decided to find a weekend place near the ocean north of San Francisco, since mountains were Garret's first love and the sea, mine. Bodega Bay is a small fishing village where salmon and crab and tourists form the center of life. We found a beautiful piece of land for sale, but the 36 acres was more than we wanted or could afford. We persuaded the somewhat "flaky" owner to divide it into four pieces, and in 1971 we bought the choice piece, sure that we would have no very near neighbors.

The land was not only beautiful but also historic. We found a wooden cross standing near the front of our section with a bronze plaque reading approximately "Here lie 300 Indians brought here by the Russians in 1812." The plaque is said to be original although the cross is clearly not. It seems that a group of Russians, about a hundred, came south from Alaska to hunt sea otter, bringing with them about 80 Aleuts. They established on the coast Fort Ross, and came inland a few miles to set up a farm. We were assured the 300 Indians were not likely to haunt the land since they apparently died of natural causes. When we were in Moscow several years later Garret tried without much success to learn more about this Russian expedition to California.

Our eight and a half acres lay off the road and up a gentle hill with a bumpy dirt path to the top. Behind that, the land fell away much more sharply through a forest of bay trees and rhododendron bushes down to Salmon Creek. The fish came up this Creek to spawn, each, so say the locals, protected by a game warden. Garret found an old trailer that would allow us to spend weekends here until we came to know the land better. We were delighted with the air of the place even before we discovered another of its secrets. One sunny morning we crawled out of bed in the trailer and set about our usual walk around our domain when suddenly we were surrounded. We dared not move for fear of hurting one of the thousands of Monarch butterflies all around us, all flying on their journey southward. Wonder at the beauty was succeeded by joy at the privilege of being there.

Even before we had plans for a house Garret set out to become part of the community. An opportunity arose when the principal owner of the general store decided to sell out and offered us the chance to buy it. It was certainly not a particularly wise investment from a purely financial point of view, but paid dividends of a different kind. We came to know some of the people of Bodega, in particular two artists who owned an old creamery that they used as a studio. Also we came to know the fishermen who not only often gave us salmon but also invited us to the "blessing of the fleet" complete with its crab cioppino feast.

Our idea was to build a small house ourselves, and we chose a place for the house in a clear area just above the steep woods. Our first step was to build a small water tower. We could have used all Noah's family in the construction, but did have two of Garret's sons to help in putting up the heavy beams that supported it all. As for the rest, we did it! Garret found an old schoolhouse window about eight feet tall that would fill the place with light, but there was a problem in installing it. After considerable thought Garret threw a rope over the beam on the top, added a pulley, attached the rope to the top of the window, and with me at the bottom to prevent the whole thing crashing down, hauled the window up. What a triumph!

My part in this whole project was part executive artistic consultant and part unskilled—very unskilled—labor. The labor part was hard work, but the rewards made it worthwhile, not just in the finished product but in the successes along the way. The sight of the window in place although there were as yet no walls, the soft, thumping sound when the tongue in one redwood board slid into the groove of the next, and the smell of the sawdust as each board was cut: all were new experiences for me.

We decided to find a local architect to design the house. We told him that we were going to build it ourselves, and that I, as executive artistic consultant, wanted a structure that looked like a Spanish mission except with large windows. After an interminable wait he presented us with a thrilling design. The first step of course was to choose the exact position for the house and to lay it out precisely using surveyors' tools. We hopped about like two children on the day when we found we had done it— off at the end by 1/8 of an inch.

And then came pouring the concrete for the footings, during which project I spent a lot of time on my knees smoothing the concrete, and thinking. Our anxiety and exhaustion were leading to more and more squabbling, in part because my capacity for following orders was limited. We agreed ultimately that it was either the house or the marriage, and the choice was clear.

We began asking around for some one qualified to take over the building project and found him in an unlikely place. We had heard about a group of talented people living nearby in a so-called "commune." Actually we had met one of their number, Serge, because he had left two of his sculptures on our land— remarkable creatures made of metal, one a very large ant and another an even larger pterodactyl. He introduced us to the group that was unlike any we had ever known. They made me a bit nervous but Garret was entirely at ease until we went to their spring cookout to roast a goat, and large numbers of them casually took off their clothes. The man who seemed to be the leader, Gary, was said to be an expert builder and metalworker. Now that I think of it we were fortunate that he was both, and also a reliable and imaginative worker. He took over the building with help from his friends and from Garret, while I made a large embroidered hanging and Moorish-style tiles for the stair risers and generally stayed out from underfoot.

As we confronted all the problems, and there were more, I was privileged to live in a world in which there was always some way to solve them. Garret lifted my already optimistic outlook to new certainty. It was magic.

As a break from all the problems we had a large party in Bodega. It was not an ordinary party, but rather a gathering of potters to do a large raku firing. I had recently begun working in a pottery studio in Berkeley where the owner had introduced the class to the unique Japanese kiln technique called raku. At the studio we used a gas-fired system but learned that the traditional kiln was fired by wood. I thought we might be able to do that on our land, and invited everybody to come bringing their pots ready for glaze firing. It turned into a frantic 12-hour day full of laughter, backbreaking work, and delight in the results.

Raku is dramatic in the result but especially in the process. A blazing fire is set and maintained at a high temperature in the partially open kiln. It takes a lot of wood and constant attention. A clay pot previously fired to hardness is covered with a glaze, placed cold in the red hot kiln, and cured in a very short time. When the pot reaches incandescence, and a beautiful sight it is, the time has come to pluck it out with tongs, drop it into a garbage can filled with dry leaves, clap on the lid, and wait until the smoke has died down. Next the pot, if still in one piece, is plunged into a bucket filled with cold water. The object of all this is to deny the glaze oxygen as it sets the leaves on fire, producing unpredictable and sometimes spectacular results. A good time was had by all, and there were even some pots that survived and made the effort worthwhile. It must have been quite a scene as dusk fell on the crowd of us scurrying around the blazing fire, surrounded by smoke, and giddy from exhaustion.

By 1971 Amy was off at UC Santa Cruz, and Mary was just beginning to cope with being a teenager in Berkeley. Amy had navigated the waters quite successfully, but her sister was another story. As she was about to begin junior high school we thought some major change might help her—and us. We heard about a new school that could only exist in California of the 1970s. The couple starting the school seemed responsible and qualified, and their plans for a boarding school physically like a summer camp and academically free-form were appealing. In the fall of 1972 we took Mary there, all three of us hoping this would be both a solution for us and an adventure for her.

(At this point I should add a few final words about my dear girls, but only a few, because their stories are their own to be told in their own way. Amy has had a successful career as a primary school counselor and a happy marriage just a year ago. Mary and I have continued to have a somewhat stormy relationship, but beneath it lies an unshakable love. She has three daughters, my grandchildren, Jessica Nan, Sara, and Aliya—and I only wish I knew them better.)

And so in the spring of 1973 Amy and Mary were away from home, and our house in Bodega was in more capable hands than ours. Sean, the red setter, had mellowed with age and loved the freedom of the country. The stage was set for a major adventure in our lives.

USSR, April-June 1973

PRE-USSR

I had heard of exchange visits by established scientists sponsored both by the American and the Soviet Academy of Sciences. I thought of applying for such a visit after I stumbled upon a book by Santha Rama Rau about her travels to the Soviet Union with her husband who was studying Soviet ballet. So it was not only out of scientific motives but also "tourist" curiosity that I applied. Little did we know what a unique opportunity this was.

I had finished my large survey of interstellar neutral hydrogen in our galaxy and thought I might try writing a monograph (similar to our article in the Reviews of Modern Physics) that would be a review of our knowledge of the interstellar medium. Information about the work in progress in the Soviet Union on the subject was very slow in coming due to the normal delay in publishing exacerbated by the need for translation into English. I knew of some of the theoretical work done by Soviet scientists but almost nothing about their observational programs. I thought that finding out directly about their contribution would make for a more balanced final product. This was indeed a good reason to go, if not the real reason.

Garret and I decided to fly to New York from San Francisco and to go in style across the ocean on the last voyage of the French cruise ship S.S. France. This gala trip went from New York to Cannes for the film Festival. So in addition to eating (often and elegantly) we saw many of the movies about to be shown at the Festival. It was for us another world—and we were about to enter yet another one.

MOSCOW AT FIRST

To call our trip to the USSR an "adventure" is to make light of it. Instead it was so profound an experience that I am daunted at the prospect of recounting it. In remembering, I see a pattern that seems to tie together our 90 individual days in the Soviet Union of 1973. Throughout most of them we skimmed the surface of the infinitely complex and subtle society in which we found ourselves. There were occasions, however, on which we saw the reality—a people of great generosity and humor living under a system that was stifling to the human spirit within.

In trying to tell this story I shall rely on both my own recollection and Garret's daily journal. His point of view differs from mine, both because it often did and because much of my time and energy went into my scientific mission. He enriched my experience in the Soviet Union, and I hope his journal will enrich my writing about it. Passages in italics come from his journal.

Almost as soon as we were airborne we learned the weather would prevent our going straight to Moscow, and that we would stop in Warsaw. A precipitous descent through gray clouds led to a bumpy landing on a gray and black and wet runway. Shepherded to a bleak building we wet sheep looked about in docile bewilderment at a colorless, sparsely furnished enclosure where we were told to wait. I'm sure my imagination was running away with me, but the whole alien surroundings with the attendant uniformed men (KGB??) led me to wonder about the wisdom of continuing. After an hour we were led again to the plane where we took off into weather that looked no better than when we came.

The Moscovites we've had any dealings with have upset most of our preconceptions in the 20 hours since we got off the plane. Customs inspector, desk clerk, waitress (all women) smiled back, put up with our poor Russian, and did their best to meet our needs. Men in the Metro trains—would they be fellow-travelers?—insisted on our taking their seats, went out of their way to help us to the right transfer, and watched Nan closely to be sure she was real.

FIRST SCIENCE

Navigating in Moscow was hazardous at best because there were no reliable beacons; the river meandered through the city in sweeping curves, and large buildings that might orient one were duplicated (exactly) in different places. So for my first visit to the Sternberg Institute of the University of Moscow, my host institution, Solomon Borisovich Pikel'ner, came to guide me there from our hotel. We had met earlier at Harvard when he came on his only visit to the United States in 1957. I was a graduate student and had the privilege of driving him out to the radio astronomy observatory so that we had a little time to become acquainted. I, of course, knew his work in theoretical astrophysics and cosmology. On the drive I asked him his impression of the United States from his brief visit. His reply surprised me. "It's so bright; the colors almost hurt my eyes." Now I saw why he said it—Moscow was so uniformly gray.

When I heard from the Soviet Academy of Science that Solomon would be my principal contact with the scientific community, I was very glad, but I could not know that he would become a friend to us both. He was a tall, slender man with short, very white hair and deep blue eyes, the whole impression being one of self-effacing gentleness. I cannot imagine him raising his voice in anger. And there were things he could be angry about—he was a Jew. In the Soviet Union of 1973 that meant both petty and significant discrimination. I learned from him that only a small number of Jews were admitted to the University, and it was most egregious that he, a world-renowned astrophysicist, was not a member of the Soviet Academy of Sciences. (Life for Solomon and his wife and daughter would have been very different with the membership: a better apartment, a car, the right to care in the academy hospital, and assured entrance into the University for his daughter.) Of course, I did not learn all this until much later.

Perhaps an excerpt from the report to the National Science Foundation I wrote at the end of my visit best describes my impression of the Russian astronomical community.[35]   Of course, this report is a formal document and does not fully express my feelings.

"I found, in general, an open and welcoming attitude, and not only from the Russian scientists I already knew. There were, however, some problems: making arrangements to visit with a particular scientist was annoying or worse, despite the fact that the institute was quite open to visitors. Part of the problem certainly arose from the extreme crowding in offices at the institute; in order to work, an astronomer normally stayed at home, and it was therefore necessary to make an appointment well in advance, usually a week. Also, most of the prominent scientists are extraordinarily busy with duties other than research and teaching—editing, committee meetings, oral examinations for graduate students from all over the Soviet Union, and many others of which I am not fully aware. As a result, my hours of fruitful consultation were incredibly limited, despite a growing persistence on my part.

The content of those hours was also (to be frank) surprisingly uninteresting. With the exception of one man (who is no longer in full-time research) the junior scientists seem to be doing a reasonably competent job without a vision of where their work fits into the larger picture, and with no thought at all of directing their efforts in new directions. (The contrast with staff members and students at Berkeley is beyond description.) Unfortunately, the senior scientists are not engaged in a more than peripheral way in the study of the interstellar medium. As with all things in the Soviet Union, there are qualifications to be made to such a flat statement. Dr. Pikel'ner, for example, and Dr. Kaplan (who lives in Gorky, a city closed to foreigners?) have written an article for an American review journal concerning the influence of galactic-scale dynamics on the interstellar gas."

I saw some women among the graduate students but none (or very, very few) in positions of real independence. Only part of the problem was discrimination; there was also the practical problem of maintaining a home and family in this city where nothing seems to be set up to save time.

With some difficulty I was able to arrange to visit the Lebedev Physical Institute's Serpakov Radio Observatory.[36] Unfortunately the day set for the visit was very stormy, with gusts of wind straight from Siberia driving the stinging rain. The trip provided the most striking demonstration of the outdated nature of Soviet astronomical equipment, and led me to a greater appreciation of the effort required for a Soviet observational astronomer to produce meaningful results. The 25-meter radio telescope at the site has an altitude-azimuth mounting, not unusual in large instruments of this type, that can follow an astronomical source across the sky only by changing positions in two coordinates. I unwisely accepted an invitation to observe the tracking mechanism—unwise because I had to climb an outside slippery, steel staircase to reach the perch high up inside the telescope, where the observer guides the instrument by keeping a star on a pair of cross hairs. No professional radio telescope in the U.S. operated in such a fashion then; computer control of such a system was considered (rightly) to be absolutely essential.

AMERICAN EMBASSY

The building that houses the American Embassy looks like what it very likely was at some time in the past—a municipal office with driveways into a rear courtyard. In the States a big-city Girl Scouts Center would think it beneath their dignity. Each of the three entrances is policed by one or two pleasant militiamen —Moscow's finest—who make sure that only U.S. citizens go in. (One of my favorite photographs from the trip is one that Garret took of one of these militiaman as he was protesting, "No, no! Take a picture of her—she's prettier that I am.")

We have a great advantage over the people who come here as tourists, because we may eat at, grocery-shop at, and have our washing done at the Embassy. It would be hard to rank the three privileges, but the excellence of the dinner—served at the mid-day and inexpensive—makes many of the exchange people one-meal-a-day addicts ... When mail, general information, Metro maps, money transfer, and feeling of background security are added to those, it is obvious that the Embassy does a service that is almost impossible to put a value on. (In addition, of great importance to us was access to the International Herald-Tribune, because in the spring of 1973 we got all our information about the Watergate investigation from the few columns accorded it in the international newspaper.) I imagine that the Embassy has some political purposes, too, but they almost disappear in the nearer picture of creature comfort.

Ironically, it was the Embassy that revealed to us a glimpse of Soviet reality. Solomon and his wife had invited Dr. Kaplan and us to dinner one evening. While we were having lunch, I realized I was uncertain whether Dr. Kaplan was going to come to get us or not. Since I had Solomon's telephone number (there was no Moscow telephone directory!) I used the pay phone in the Embassy to ask him. The three of us arrived together, and as Solomon opened the door I realized something was very wrong. His face registered a mixture of fear and extreme embarrassment. His first words to me were, "Don't ever do that again." As he saw my bewildered face he added, "Don't ever call here again from the Embassy." My protest that it was from a pay telephone was met by a look of incredulity at my naiveté. My immediate expression of profound regret was met with, "I made it all right, but please don't do it again." I have no idea how he "made it all right," but it can't have been pleasant.

As we were sitting around the table, the Watergate scandal came up. The Russians' reaction was, "What's all the fuss about? That kind of thing happens all the time." My reply was, "Not in MY country!" I'm sure they thought me a hopeless babe-in-the-woods.

"No, no! Take a picture of her—she's prettier than I am."

GETTING ABOUT

Spring is here now and, though the trees don't admit it yet, there are flower sellers in the tunnels that cross under wide squares to compete with the small book-stalls, lottery-ticket hawkers and postcard merchants. Now and again a reckless overcoat flaps unbuttoned, and most of the fur caps have slunk into whatever corners they hibernate in for the warm months. Sunday was a stately day—no rushing about, but a relaxed saunter, even in the Metro—much standing around in small groups; park paths dry enough for today's carriages, each with a little Moscovite attended by an unhurried father who had exchanged his <u>partfiel</u> for a pram.

Getting about in the city of Moscow without benefit of tour guide presents a real challenge. We never found such a thing as a bus schedule or map, so that *without the continued kindness of the people of Moscow we should have been hopelessly lost. Examples of that kindness abound: the woman who came to us on the bus and, somehow, made us understand that we were headed into uncharted space—dressing the driver down in the process—the militia man in the Metro, the continued insistence that I take someone's seat, all partake of the same climate. On the bus they help each other (and us) make change for the fare-box, pass fare and tickets back and forth through the crowded car, put up with the indecision of the aged even when it means missing getting off at their proper stop. And stops can be miles apart.*

There was, however, the ever-present feeling that all these people wanted more than anything was to remain anonymous and unnoticed. On the street and on the buses and trams there was no light-hearted chatter and no laughter. The rows of seated people would not look at us, although it was obvious we were foreigners. My impression was again of gray, a sight I found indescribably sad.

During our first month our social calendar was full to overflowing. We got tickets to all sorts of performances with no trouble at all and were overwhelmed with invitations from Russian scientists. I'm sure it was during the first week that we were urged to go to an ice hockey game (a first for both of us). We were both very cold and mystified by the action until the Germans (East of course) defeated the Poles. In recognition their flag was raised to the music of Deutschland uber Alles, bringing the crowd (all but two) to its feet. I could not stand; the echo of times past was too clear.

The other night we were invited out to dinner by the Ginzburgs, Vitali and Nina. We'd been coached on the Russian habit of making small gifts to our host at such times, so we went prepared—we thought. A scarf from Nan's very particular favorite YenYen, a line drawing of the Bridge, and an abalone shell that we'd made into a candle. Barely in the door, Nina started showing me her collection of old icons, knowing my special interest and, in the process, gave me a wonderful small bas relief of St. Nicholas.... As Nan said, it was a perfect way to accept me into a group that already had a common interest.

The ballet on Saturday, taking the Pikeln'ers. (We had learned that it was impossible for the ordinary Russian to obtain tickets for such a performance, and it was a special treat we could offer them.) ... The hall was a revelation; immense spaces—level after level of acre-big foyers walled in glass that framed the Kremlin towers; escalators that carried you up from one surprising floor to another and ended at a "bufet" that filled the top storey. There were tables of champagne (Russian champagne is about as good as some of the California), open-faced sandwiches, ice cream and chocolates. Then more tables with white tablecloths around which the people stood eating; all on a series of terraces around what must normally have been a dance floor. The ballet itself was all I had hoped it would be.

SHKLOVSKY

Among the Russians I came to know, by far the most intriguing
was I. S. Shklovsky, in a way because he seemed so "Western,"
and yet also so Russian. Despite his position as one of the
world's great astrophysicists he was able to join his colleagues
only on the rare occasions when he was able to leave the Soviet
Union or when they were allowed to visit Moscow. He was a
Jew and, even more threatening, a free spirit.

I came to know his work because one of his major interests was
the study of radio radiation from supernovae and quasars. He
found the mechanism for production of this radiation, a major
discovery. I met him first in 1967 at an International
Astronomical Union meeting in Prague where there was a large
Russian group. Soon after we met he enjoyed a joke at my
expense with such obvious delight that I could only laugh as
well. He said "Oh, I have someone I want you to meet." And
with that, produced (like a rabbit out of hat) a young, very handsome man. "This is Nikolai Kardashev!" The expression on my
face must have been very funny, because I had expected the
famous astronomer to be far older and far more forbidding.

There was of course more to the Russian scientist than his obvious playful nature. I knew this when he pointed out the Prague
ghetto with the statement, "You must go there." I did and I shall
never forget it. The cemetery was filled to overflowing with
tombstones leaning against one another in a tumble of tragedy.
The old synagogue was a shattering memorial with the names of
famous concentration camps emblazoned high on the walls and
the names of thousands of victims listed all over them. Outside,
up an outdoor stairway, lay a small gallery of drawings made by
the children of the ghetto. Words could never describe it.

In about 1970 Shklovsky and V. L.Ginzburg were allowed to
visit the astronomy department of UC Berkeley.[37] Garret and I

were lucky enough to entertain them in our home and to take them to San Francisco to buy gifts. They were awe struck at the riches available to anyone and chose with considerable difficulty. In a women's clothing store Shklovsky spotted a long, hooded loden cape that he insisted I model and then insisted I buy because I looked so Russian. (He was delighted when I wore it in Moscow.) During dinner in a favorite San Francisco restaurant he told a complicated story about animals that I do not now remember, but I do have the small napkin on which he drew clever sketches of some geese, a rabbit, a pig, and a porcupine. After dinner we walked around the city a little, and when we paused at a street corner Shklovsky was approached by another pedestrian with a request for directions. He turned, hopping with pleasure, to say, "You see, they think I'm an American!"

Our visit to Moscow gave me the opportunity to bring Shklovsky something he was not allowed to come to Berkeley to get. It was the 1972 Bruce Medal of the Astronomical Society of the Pacific, an honor bestowed each year on a distinguished astronomer. The president of the Society charged me with setting up a suitable ceremony for the presentation. At Shklovsky's home institute (the Sternberg) we assembled a large group of his colleagues and friends and several representatives from the American Embassy. On the blackboard I had made a list of past years with the previous winners. For 1972 I left the winner blank until I had presented the medal, with a very brief, very simple speech in Russian (!) That evening he gave a party to celebrate where there was much food and drink and exchange of gifts—altogether a lively time. Our gift to him was a fiber-optic "fountain" popular at the time. My surprise gift was a small traditional witch made of rough twine, complete with babushka and broom. It was, of course, a source of merriment, and still makes me smile.

Through all his infectious humor it was clear that Shklovsky was greatly saddened by the conditions in his country. For instance I know that he resented the fact that his colleague and friend, Sam Kaplan, was forced to live outside Moscow in the restricted city of Gorky. On the other hand he felt a real love for his homeland and had no intention of leaving it.

Adding Shklovsky's name to the list of Bruce Medalists. Left to right: Prof. D. Ya. Martynov, Prof. I. S. Shklovsky, and Nan Dieter Conklin.

ARMENIA

HOSPITAL

On Sunday Solomon called to remind us of our planned walk in the country. We went to the end of the metro line and a couple of miles on the bus to a birch forest on the outskirts of town. Real quiet with some birds and real bugs walking around. Pikelner and Zoya were good, quiet company; she wove a halo of yellow wildflowers with the help of a few strands of Nan's hair. It was a peaceful day, but soon after we got home I noticed a small blister on my knee that we treated with disinfectant and a band-aid. Although by Monday morning it wasn't any better, we had no time to see the Embassy doctor before our trip to Armenia, Crimea, and the North Caucuses.

My conferences in Armenia were interrupted for the visit of a local doctor, summoned to examine my obviously infected knee. She was young and gentle and to my surprise recommended a local remedy: application of several large leaves, plantain, I think. She said it often worked and was worth a try. When the next morning there was no improvement, she said with some regret that I really should go to the hospital in Yerevan. So she and Xrant Tovmassian, our host astronomer, came along with Garret and me on a journey that was to give us a glimpse of the real Soviet Union.

On the two hour journey our country doctor explained that this was a hospital under construction. As we approached it we were surprised to see a large crowd of people struggling to get in. Once again we were embarrassed by being ushered into the building ahead of all these people. After a short consultation with our doctor, a woman I assumed to be a nurse led me down the hall about 50 or 60 feet to a somewhat larger room on the other side. It contained on the left a sort of examining table and on the right another long table with a green cloth on it. My alarm increased when I saw that there was an array of surgical instruments on that table. Being in a makeshift operating room was cause enough for concern, but in addition I was aware that it was far from sterile. At the nurse's bidding I climbed up on the table, and it was then I realized that my small command of Russian would be of no use; she was speaking Armenian. Panic was ready to pounce!

After some interminable minutes a middle-aged man came in whom I did not recognize at first as the doctor, because he, like the nurse, wore no surgical clothing. I remember being particularly disturbed for some reason that neither had anything on their heads. (Perhaps I had seen too many TV operating rooms.) The doctor approached my very sore knee, and then said something unintelligible to the nurse. She walked to the other table and chose a scalpel. Now I was aware that I was a foreign visitor and should conduct myself with dignity. However, when he made a move that was obviously precursor to cutting my leg, I screamed first "No!", and when that brought no response, "Stop!" That did it. His annoyance was obvious; his response was to go to a nearby cabinet, choose a hypodermic needle, and inject its contents directly into the wound. For a little while I didn't know what was happening, but soon realized he was cutting away the infected flesh.

When he was finished they applied a rather large bandage, and made me understand that I should come back in a few days. Obviously I had no intention of doing so. The doctor left and the nurse indicated I should get up. She led me to the door, and as we turned down the hall someone called to her. She left me standing there on very unsteady legs, but I was able to make my way back to the waiting room. When I opened the door Garret looked at me and said with alarm, "What happened?" The doctor immediately helped me to lie down on the couch, took my pulse (for the first time in this hospital), and made me understand how sorry she was to have brought me here. My experience was made far worse by going out through the crowd desperate to get in.

My leg took a long time to heal, and the experience is with me still in sharp focus. When we got back to Moscow, I saw the embassy doctor. He was not as shocked at my description as I had imagined, because he had heard many similar stories. I continue to think of those people struggling to get in.

OBSERVATORY

However, for me the pursuit of my astronomical mission was for the first time fun. The atmosphere at the Bjurakan Astrophysical Observatory in Armenia was one of dedicated effort with apparently better optical telescopes and great hope for the performance of a new one under construction. The group was obviously dominated by Professor Viktor Ambartsumian, its director. I was impressed, however, by the energy and imagination of various members of the staff. The radio astronomical project at Bjurakan apparently failed to work because of long delays in getting parts and engineering help. The one radio astronomer on the staff, an imaginative young man, traveled extensively "outside" to get his material. He now contemplated an infrared program at Bjurakan—I thought, "and he may even bring it about!"

This is a separate country that joins the Soviet Union; the people look different from Moscovites, are more Latin in temperament, more full of life, less—what? Maybe less affected or formal. The language is entirely different from Russian and many people here know both tongues; the village houses are stone— unpainted—so they are in much better repair than their counterparts to the north. Right now the fruit trees are in blossom and the Observatory is full of daffodils and tulips with rose-bushes on the brink of putting out buds. The terrain is hilly; there's snow on the high places and, above all, there's Ararat. Above all in every sense. You tend to look along at a high level to find this mountain, 40 or so miles away and across the Turkish frontier, and then find that it's up in the sky, hanging without support, a mass of snow that reaches more than 12,000 feet above the plain that Yerevan is built on.

Sunday morning Xrant, Angela [Xrant's wife], Nan and I went to the cathedral at Echmiadzin where a crowd of spectators wandered in and out while priest, deacon, and acolytes chanted their way through the mass. Outside the building several of the worshipers had a live rooster or two hanging head-down and we were told that these (and sometimes a sheep) were offered as sacrifices, the cooked results then being distributed to any of the onlookers who were hungry. The entire combination seemed to us more voodoo than Christian.

BACK TO MOSCOW

With some considerable regret we left Armenia to return to Moscow where we found our situation in one way quite different from when we left. Before, we had been overwhelmed with invitations and entertainments, but now we found ourselves much more on our own. Almost no tickets were available to us from the office in the hotel. The change was so great that we felt it was a matter of policy and not of chance—an evidence of how much our visit was "orchestrated."

For me the situation was frustrating because my goal of locating people whose work might be of interest to me was growing increasingly elusive. I was finding that the Soviet astronomical community—at least the observational part—was at least ten years behind us. It seemed apparent to me that the problem was one of outdated equipment with no improvement in sight.

With time to spare I accepted an invitation from Sue, the wife of an American scientist, to visit Moscow's Palace of Pioneers. She was an elementary school teacher and therefore particularly interested in how the Soviet Union educated its children through the Pioneer movement (said to be similar to our Scouts). The building where they met was of the ostentatious variety, like the metro and the Palace of Congresses, with lots of marble floors, all sparkling clean. The building was full of children from 7 to 14, all dressed in black and white uniforms with red scarves at the neck. I say "full of children" although one would never have known it by the pervasive silence. They were working in small groups on a wide variety of projects—as diverse as embroidery and space flight, and including cooking, photography, metal-and wood-working, and more. The results were truly astonishing in their complexity and precision. Sue and I were unable during the tour to exchange views, but were very quick to do so outside. We both felt the experience to be oddly and profoundly depressing. Somehow the absence of the joy and freedom of childhood was almost too much to bear.

CRIMEA

We next visited the Crimean Astrophysical Observatory. I knew that its work in radio astronomy was largely concerned with the sun, but there were two or three men working in areas that promised to be of some interest to me. However, although my visit was planned many months in advance, and cleared a few days before my arrival, those men were not at the Observatory.

Here in the Crimea Nan's knee has been improving, and it has been possible for her to soak almost all the original packing off —the tub is immense and this morning there was water warm enough to be comfortable in.

I suppose that 24 hours is too short a time to make judgments, but this place has much more the feeling of Moscow than did Bjurakan. Wednesday night, at 8, we went to the Gershberg's for dinner and slides. If the Chinese saying about a picture of being worth 1000 words has any truth in it, we are now in the position of two over-stuffed encyclopedia. Solomon, Kurt, these two and I don't know how many more have trotted out the little 10r projector and the results of hundreds of hours of photography—maybe in an effort to show us that all the Soviet Union wasn't like wherever we were at that minute.

We were pretty happy at the prospect of the weekend to ourselves in Yalta after a short stop at the radio astronomy Observatory in Simez. It really isn't possible to describe our horror at hearing Galanski say—in response to Nan's question about places to eat, "Viktor will show you the restaurants; he's going to stay with you and bring you back Sunday." The court favorite who was presented with a white elephant couldn't have been more disgusted than we. Besides that, it was raining hard; the clouds were within a few feet of the ground and if a good fairy and turned up with three wishes, mine would have been home, home, home. Through the exercise of diplomacy that would have made an English Ambassador jealous, we managed to reduce the term to Saturday morning from 11 to 2.

SEVERNY KAFKAS

OBSERVATORY

Early in June we set out on our next trip out of Moscow—and the time when we felt happiest in the Soviet Union. We went to the Severny Kafkas (North Caucasus) Mountains to see the new six-meter optical telescope, then the largest in the world. We were the first Americans to visit it, a truly unforgettable experience. The observatory was in stunningly beautiful surroundings, with Mt. Elbrus (18,000 ft) visible on a clear day, and the main ridge of the Caucasus nearby. The telescope was in a beautiful building, the interior of marble and stained glass, designed with taste not discernable elsewhere in the Soviet Union. It was obviously intended as a national monument.

The Observatory is really something to behold: the first level has a stained glass ceiling that slowly comes into focus as a representation of the 12 signs of the zodiac—stylized and catching the imagination with images that grew from the world's first astronomers. Offices, dormitories, and single rooms surround the central core that will hold the world's largest and most complete optical telescope. One quadrant on the second level is furnished with the works of artists from across the country, but the core of the work is the instrument that will be the six meter telescope—without mirror as yet but an awe-inspiring machine. What is unusual is the combination of artistry that brings together scientific professionalism and the softer reach of man's search for meaning that has built the discipline that is astronomy.

The telescope mounting was impressive, and the attendant computers, re-aluminizing facilities, and living quarters for observers, were first-class. The mirror had not been delivered because of problems with its final figuring. They had hopes, (although somewhat faint), of reaching an image size of

0.5 seconds of arc. (A point source, a star, would appear to be this large due to the atmosphere and the imperfections of the instrument.) I was surprised at this modest goal for the telescope when I learned that on some occasions the atmosphere would allow one to achieve values substantially smaller. However, even the director was concerned about the weather on the mountain. When we were there for a week in early June, it rained every afternoon with high, billowing clouds, and cleared somewhat by evening. On two nights I saw a spectacular display of stars against an absolutely black sky. Marvelous, but not available a large percentage of the time. Winter was said to be better.

The scientific secretary gave us the grand tour; and a lesson about preconceptions, for we had thought that scientific secretaries were bureaucrats who didn't know much about science or people. I started to take off my hiking boots in deference to the marble floors and he knelt and laced them up! I'm sure he did more to soften my feeling about the people of the USSR than anything that had taken place since we've been here—and it was an unselfconscious action that had no relation to nationalities or ideologies. He was a short, unprepossessing man who was pleased with his Observatory, and who had a built-in feeling about the value of persons that was hard to define. There wasn't anything either subservient or overbearing in anything he did. He works for the Soviet Union, and he works for science in general—he's proud (rightly) of the Observatory and its possibilities, but not to the detriment of people as individuals.

The development of radio astronomy at the Special Astronomical Observatory (at Leningrad and in the North Caucasus) was again dependent on the energy of one man, Yurii Parijskii, Vice-Director of SAO. The facilities at Leningrad were dreadfully outdated and certainly severely handicapped by the presence, within sight, of Leningrad Airport. The work there on interstellar neutral hydrogen, still in progress, was at least fifteen years out-of-date, and had already been completed elegantly at Berkeley. However, a new instrument modeled on the one in Leningrad was being built at Zelinchukskaya. The design was novel and the construction involved some risk because of the high precision required.

It consists of a circle 600 meters in diameter outlined by 15 foot high supports. Each of these brackets holds an aluminum plate 2 m.x 7-1/2 m. That can be made to rotate in three directions— they are nominally vertical with the long axis 90 degrees to the ground and so form a continuous band 7-1/2 m. high with the bottom edge 3m from the ground. The notion is that they can be tilted to observe different pieces of sky.

The RATAN-600 telescope was about one-quarter complete when we saw it.[38] An unfortunate problem was that no money was available for providing computer control of the positioning (in three dimensions) of the panels. In order to change the direction of pointing of the telescope, the individual electric motors controlling each panel had to be activated by hand—and there were about 900 of them. Parijskii took us to see it and his enthusiasm, patience, and faith in the concept made him a very interesting guide. Moreover his plan for making the machine available to outside astronomers seemed to give the Observatory a direction, perhaps a philosophy, that promised good things for its future. (Not, I fear, fully realized.)

I treasure our visit to Zelenchukskaya for the beauty and serenity of its mountains and the warmth and generosity of its remarkable people. *Nan's birthday, June 10, came on Sunday before the day we were to leave and the permanent residents made a party. There was fresh trout, champagne, greens, cordials, and "silyotka," topped off with a cake and konyak. It was a happy enough occasion that even some strong criticism by*

Vitya/Sasha/Mikael and my equally energetic responses didn't lead to any real unpleasantness. At midnight Jean-Claude wanted to see the big telescope so we made a two-hour tour.

We saw the observer's cage, apparently ready and waiting for the great mirror, and our guide shyly offered us the chance to try out the chair. Jean-Claude Pecker, my colleague from Paris, was visiting Severny Kafkas at the same time we were, and he and I were thrilled to be the first foreigners to sit there inside the great telescope.

The next day in stark contrast I came upon a person from another time. As I rested beside a mountain road, a small man on a pony approached me, and as I stood to greet him I was met with a dazzling smile. My Russian greeting brought more smiles and a brief, friendly conversation. (At that moment I blessed every hour I had struggled over the Russian language.) On the way back we visited his home, a large tent made of skins where he offered us a drink (of uncertain origin), and offered to bring fresh milk for tomorrow's breakfast. It was for moments like these that we traveled.

It was difficult to say goodbye to these people who were relaxed and generous and simply fun. We left behind a few mementos: kitchen utensils and wooden plaque holding an example of each American coin (Garret's creation). Maya hung up the plaque in the spacious kitchen where I hope it still hangs. Next day Vitya drove us to the airport at Mineralni Vodi for the trip back to Moscow. The ride down the mountain was enough to take our minds off our sadness. Going down the steep, narrow road at an alarming speed was a lot more frightening than the trip up a week ago. The journey found Garret *wishing all the time that I'd drunk less vodka, led a better life, stayed home, walked, or had the courage to ask the driver to slow down.*

LENINGRAD

Thursday night we took the Red Arrow to Leningrad, a remarkable train, where one can easily imagine Peter the Great speeding to St. Petersburg in comfortable luxury. In addition, he required the road bed for the train to be flat so as not to disturb his slumber. All night we blessed the great czar.

In Leningrad we had the strangest of all of our experiences in the Soviet Union. We got to the very large hotel where they served us a breakfast of sorts in a large nearly deserted dining room. Garret and I ate the same unappetizing dishes, and dragged ourselves up to the room—or at least I "dragged." Garret was ready for a walk around the city to find the Hermitage. I was about to lie down when the "djernia" came to the door. She made polite noises, and then to my astonishment offered to trade my dollars for rubles at the black market price. (A little background: the legal exchange rate at $1.30/ruble was nothing short of highway robbery, but we had been warned of the risk in dealing on the black market. It would have been the height of folly to do so with someone obviously an official, even a lowly one.) At my refusal she seemed disappointed and left me alone.

By this time I was quite sleepy, lay down, and fell fast asleep. Within what seemed a moment, I heard someone calling and then shaking me. I struggled through a great heaviness to come awake and then to stay awake. I am absolutely convinced that I had been drugged—as convinced today as I was that afternoon.

My memory of Leningrad includes the sight of beautiful wrought iron work on balconies of private houses and on bridges over the canals (virtually all exceedingly dusty). We went together to the Hermitage with considerable anticipation because we knew of its great collections. The handsome façade facing the harbor was marred by the dirty, peeling yellow paint. Inside it seemed that every inch of the walls from floor to ceiling was covered with paintings, very close together, and without adequate lighting. I remember especially peering at a van Gogh I had never seen before, longing to have a flashlight.

We've been trying to describe to ourselves the total feeling we have about the Soviet Union, but there isn't a clear-cut answer to why we react as we do. In my terms I think I find it a God-less of nation, not in the sense that many of the people at home are God-less, but rather that this people is a-theistic by policy. In the U.S. a large percentage of the nation act against the teachings of the Judeo-Christian belief, but that belief is there, forming a background of law against which every one judges himself. Here the teaching is that no God exists and the rude-ness, the total absence of concern by car drivers, the absence of pride in a job, the wooden approach to learning by all but a very few, the retreat into drunkenness by the discouraged are all natural consequences of the teaching that man is the final arbiter   that he owes no allegiance to anything better then the state, itself only a mass of men.

Bad leaders, a czar or a Hitler, can ruin a country in spite of its religion, but a country whose religion is anti-religion is spoiled in a worse way for there its soul is defective, and man has denied the thing that above all others separates him from bes-tiality. (I am ashamed to say that at first I left out this paragraph from Garret's journal. I did not share Garret's beliefs, and am reminded that he never for a moment challenged my view of the world. A remarkable man, my husband.)

Our weariness with this whole enterprise became apparent on a small trip we took out of Leningrad. We went to the czar's Summer Palace on a boat filled to overflowing with pushy, noisy Russian tourists. Along with them and the ever present talking guide we toured the lavish (but slightly shabby) Palace, vowing all the while never to set foot in such a place again. Yes, it was definitely time to go home.

GETTING OUT

That's how all foreigners spoke of leaving the U.S.S.R., including diplomats simply going to Finland to shop. For us sadness clouded the relief of going home. We had made real friends, most of whom we would never see again. On the morning of our departure Solomon Borisovich Pikel'ner came to the hotel to say goodbye, and I am afraid that I embarrassed this very shy man by reaching up to hug him in farewell. He came with us to the bus that would take us to the embassy for the first step in our journey. I remember very clearly seeing in his intense blue eyes a longing for many unspoken things. (About two years later I learned that Solomon had died in the course of an appendectomy performed not at an academy hospital but at one open to Jews.)

At the airport we dared not look at one another as two colleagues, Novikov and his wife, Nina, presented us with probably the largest and certainly the ugliest vase we had ever seen. However, all was not lost. When they had left us we carefully put it under a chair and abandoned it there.

After a short wait all the passengers were shepherded into a small fenced area with an unfortunate resemblance to a cage where all passports were again examined. Foolish as it clearly was, there was a large, collective sigh when the uniformed officials were satisfied with our documents. And then, one of them opened the door out to the tarmac and the waiting, beautiful Air France plane that would carry us "out" to Paris. In another excerpt from my report to the National Science Foundation I wrote:

> "From a strictly scientific point of view, I must say (with some sorrow), that my journey was virtually useless. The current work in the Soviet Union in my field is so far behind that in the United States, that I felt

sometimes as if I had been transported back in time by
twenty or thirty years. As with every such statement
made about the Soviet Union, there are exceptions.
However, the fact remains that a prodigious expendi-
ture of time, (three months), produced only a few hours
of moderately useful discussions

From a less strictly scientific point of view, the journey
was productive. I saw Soviet astronomy at first hand—
its observatories and offices, its computers, and its telescopes. More important, of course, I spoke with many
Soviet astronomers, some of whom I had known at
meetings and as visitors in our home. My view of
Soviet publications is forever modified by that experience, in one sense by increasing my skepticism, and in
another by increasing my admiration for the occasional
first-rate work."

From a personal point of view, the journey had a profound effect
on my view of myself, my American colleagues, and my country. One has few such experiences in a lifetime. It is for this
reason that I am deeply grateful for the opportunity to visit the
Soviet Union. I found my return to Berkeley (by way of Paris),
an indescribably exciting experience. I saw everything with
fresh eyes: the vitality of astronomy as practiced in Berkeley,
the wonders of the local supermarket, and the evidences of
personal freedom everywhere. I shall not forget my joy in realizing that it is all really mine—that it is my home.

STOPOVER

Boarding that Air France plane was stepping into another world, a familiar one seen with eyes eager to remember every detail. The colorful interior, the slender, elegant stewardesses, and even the food and drink they served seemed strangely luxurious. We planned to stop overnight in Paris to break the long journey back to Berkeley. Our colleague Jean-Claude took us to one of his favorite restaurants in Paris, where he knew the owner very well. When she asked what I would like to eat, I said, "Lettuce, lots of lettuce." After I told her I'd seen nothing green to eat in three months, she brought me a very large glass bowl filled with crisp, fresh leaves. In times to come we ate often at Les Limours, but nothing of their splendid menu was better than that first taste of home.

In the morning we set out to explore but with quite different expectations. I had spent only a couple of days in Paris and wanted very much to come to know it better; Garret on the other hand had spent longer in the city than he wished when he came as a soldier in World War II, and his memories were not generally happy ones. He wanted to show me where he had slept on his previous visit—the Petit Palais, no less. It is now a museum, but the original architecture remains, including an immense glass roof over the great Hall, and it is under that expanse that he along with hundreds of others slept in wartime Paris. However, I could see as the day and evening passed that he was remembering the unique and enduring magic of Paris. I think it was his taking me to the magnificent illuminated fountains at the Palais de Chaillot that tipped the scale. We both wanted to stay a little longer and delayed our flight a couple of days.

The next day was filled with the typical light of Paris—a milky sky producing a gentle caressing glow on the ancient buildings. There was also an intangible air in the city of the hedonistic, a reveling in the beauty and elegance of its women, in the delight in well-prepared food, even the simplest fare, and in the undeniably grand mark left on the city by history. We walked the length of the Champs Elysees, or, more accurately, strolled like proper Parisians along the grand, wide sidewalk with trees overhead filtering the light and with benches inviting a rest.

As the time to leave came we thought briefly of delaying our departure again, but decided instead to come back. We had spent a long time at an intensity not common in our lives, and it was time to go home. This time it was an American plane full of our self-assured, easy-going, somewhat unruly, and familiar countrymen. The drive home to Berkeley took us over a multi-level freeway interchange that became unforgettable. High above it all flew the largest American flag I had ever seen. We were home.

Going into the house on High Court had an oddly alien feeling not only because we had been gone for more than three months, but also because we had been living such a different life.

Our next stop was Bodega to check on the progress of our house, and during the coming months we saw it fulfill the promise of its original drawings. However, some practical matters remained—for instance, water. The Creek was a long way below the house and required a substantial pump to raise the water. Garret decided that we needed to store some water closer to the house and to use a smaller pump to get it into the house. His solution was typical of his attack on such a problem. On a concrete slab below and behind the house he placed four huge wooden wine casks he found in a nearby winery. In order to clean them he had to climb up to the top and then jump down to the bottom of each of the four of them. When he spoke to me from his wooden chamber the echoing sound was hilariously funny. For quite a long time the water was slightly pink, and for even longer had a distinctly winy scent.

FORMALDEHYDE, 1971-1973

In 1969 formaldehyde (H_2CO) had been discovered in the inter-stellar gas.[39] (I find it amusing that this particular chemical, familiar to everybody in a quite different context, turns up in the interstellar gas.) It was a surprising discovery because this molecule containing four atoms is larger than any previously found, hydrogen and OH with one and two atoms respectively. This is no trivial matter because the formation of such a large molecule in the rarefied interstellar gas is difficult to explain. One place where such a thing could happen is in the distinct dark "dust" clouds that are apparent only because they absorb light from stars lying behind them. Investigating this was what took me from Bodega during the week.

In the radio spectrum formaldehyde was discovered because it absorbs radiation from bright radio sources. My survey of H2CO in dust clouds[40] depended on the molecule absorbing the very low intensity background radiation associated with the Big Bang. It was a sort of observation reasonable to do with our low-resolution antenna and high sensitivity receiver. In addi-tion, since the signal would certainly be weak, the observations would require long periods of observation time, available to me on our antenna.

Two facts were apparent in the data from this survey. One, the formaldehyde lines are all relatively weak and two, the stronger ones occur in darker dust clouds. This is about the situation one would expect, but I had grown wary of intuitive expectations.

To give you an idea of the scale of the project, of the 381 large dark dust clouds I examined, 307 showed no evidence of formaldehyde after 800 hours of observation. All the signals were weak, but even that simple fact led to a valuable conclusion. Only weak signals were observed because of the correlation between optical depth (roughly speaking, density) and excitation temperature; that is, in no cloud do we find high optical depth and low excitation temperature, because such a combination would produce a strong signal.

(I use the term "temperature," but here it needs a little explanation. "Excitation temperature" is only a measure of the strength of the signal produced in the local conditions of the cloud, and has no connection with real-world hot and cold. I find this difficult to describe, which suggests to me that I do not understand it well enough. In order to put into ordinary language a complex idea that among scientists is spoken of in the lingo of the trade, I must remember my introduction to the term, now very long ago.)

The other obvious characteristic was that stronger signals occurred from darker clouds. Less obvious but true: the stronger signals did not arise from more formaldehyde but from "colder" formaldehyde which, in a complex bit of reasoning, suggests that the H_2CO excitation arises from collisions.

There was one cloud in which the shape of the profile defied explanation. Eventually I concluded that only anomalies in the details of the molecular transition similar to those found in the OH observations would explain the result.[41] Such an unexpected conclusion could well qualify as a "zebra" while there are other possible "horses." One possible explanation is that there were two formaldehyde clouds with nearly the same velocity so that they produced a single, apparently abnormal line profile.

Incidentally, one of my colleagues at Berkeley published a paper six months later supporting the presence of a second velocity component[42]—to my surprise. In my view the configuration required was very unlikely to occur, and I could find no function with physically meaningful parameters for the two clouds.

On the other hand, no proposal for the excitation of formaldehyde in dark clouds predicts the model I suggested. It is often
true that a scientific project raises more questions than answers.

Although Garret spent some time during the week in Bodega, I
came only on weekends, where I continued "throwing pots,"
and that led to another project for Garret (I seemed to keep him
endlessly busy, but he never complained.) I needed a pottery
wheel of my own, and to my amazement he made one. He built
a small building near the Bodega house to hold not only the
wheel but also the generator and a sauna. The small white shed
had a red tile roof and a large window next to my wheel that
looked out on a beautiful clump of trees.

This was the period in which the atmosphere on the Berkeley
campus grew worse and worse. We saw so many scenes we
would never have imagined possible: a helicopter outside my
sixth floor window releasing tear gas, a policeman with night-
stick in hand chasing a girl on the walk below me, and most
memorably, along the north perimeter of the campus a line of
very young national guardsmen carrying rifles with fixed
bayonets. What had begun as campus grievances became
desperate protests against the war in Vietnam in the tradition of
students around the world. Garret and I had ambivalent feelings
about the protests because two of his sons were in Vietnam.

BACK TO FRANCE, 1974

I received an invitation to give a series of lectures in the spring of 1974 at the Collège de France in Paris. I could hardly believe my luck until I remembered that Jean-Claude was on the faculty and clearly behind the invitation. As director of the Institut d' Astrophysique he was also able to offer us use of an apartment at the Institute. In addition, as a member of the French Academy of Science, he obtained permission for us to visit the cave at Lascaux, the premier prehistoric site in France, now closed to the public. At least as important, both Jean-Claude and his wife Annie made us feel welcome in Paris and in their home.

My memory of these months has a quality very hard to put in words. It consists not only of a series of unforgettable places, but also of a harmony between us. Traveling is of course one of the hardest things two people can do together, but for each of us the experiences were intensified and deepened because we shared them. However, there was one situation which often caused friction until I figured out a solution. Garret was totally unreasonable when there was a deadline like a train or plane to catch, but I developed a tactic to cope with his impatience. I would ask him at what time I should be ready and then aimed for five minutes before that. We never missed anything.

During this trip we visited the famous cave at Lascaux, an experience that was, quite literally, unforgettable. We knew the story of its accidental discovery in 1940 when Marcel Ravidat, a schoolboy, stumbled on the cave while searching for his dog. We were met at the entrance by that boy, 34 years older but just as enthusiastic as the day he'd made the great discovery. He told us he was going to lead us into the cave in the dark. We must step carefully just behind him. He left us for a moment at a place about 30 feet inside the cave and went back to the opening to turn on the light. It was a moment I shall never forget—in fact, in some ways it changed my life.

My first sensation was of a flood of color. There were rich red, brilliant yellow, deep orange, red-brown, black, all earth colors, and overwhelming. Then I could see that these were the paintings of animals in vibrant, active life. Some were huge drawings, five or six feet across and others were small, no bigger than my hand. Many were overlapping, painted on top of one another, giving the impression of an exuberant, free spirit. Some were of animals we know well like deer and horses, and others of great animals not known in our time. All the paintings were very near us. This great Hall of the Bulls is only about 20 feet wide and 15 feet high, and it is the largest of the chambers.

Marcel began to tell us about the people who had made this magnificent scene. They lived 17,000 years ago—not here in the cave but near it. They used this hidden place for their homage to the animals of their lives, perhaps in a religious sense and perhaps not. It must have been a labor of love, involving collecting the materials for paints, finding ways to reach up to the walls, and all in a space lit only with their simple, flickering oil lamps. As we looked at the drawings in detail it was clear that there were real artists among these "primitive" people. Marcel showed us several examples of their understanding of making a three-dimensional object real in two dimensions. One that I remember well has to do with making a side view of a four-legged animal look real. In drawing the legs on the far side one simply leaves a space between the end of the lines defining the leg and the line of the belly. And that's how it's done today.

A layer of clear, calcite crystal has covered the rock wall in a way that has preserved the paintings and now gives them a glittering life. Because the layer is irregular on both a small and large-scale, the scattering of the light gives an illusion of life. In the deepest part of the cave is perhaps the most touching image of all—a child had put his hand up to the wall and an artist had sprayed paint at it, leaving the imprint behind.

I came away knowing that I wanted to try to do what they had done—capture a part of my world seen through my own eyes. Soon after, I tried making "copies" of the photographs in water-color. My attempts, of course, were a pale shadow of the originals, but making them involved very careful study of each one—all of which increased my sense of awe at what these artists accomplished so long ago.

As we wandered around Paris, said to be everyone's second home, we saw great barges on the Seine, many used as very large house boats. Garret was enchanted. "Wouldn't it be great! There would be enough room there for my tools and your pottery, and we'd be living in the middle of Paris!" I was discovering that my oh-so-practical, so organized husband was also an imaginative dreamer.

FRANCE, 1975

The major event of late 1974 in Berkeley was our finding Jacques, the first of our black standard poodles. He was also in some ways the most remarkable, and certainly the one closest to me. We had a special mutual understanding that is both rare and precious with any animal. He knew that when no one else understood what he wanted, I would.

We went back to France in the spring of 1975, and fortunately Garret kept a diary of the trip. I am quoting from Garret's diary because I had forgotten most of this. His notes, however, bring the place and the man to life.

May 25: The first stop after the hotel was the Café Daguerre where Nan filled one of her requirements by ordering strawberry tarts. Then we took bus No. 38 to the rue des Ecoles to get some guides Michelin at Gibert, found the Metro at Luxembourg has all new cars, and came back to eat a half chicken at Les Limours. Madame gave us a fine welcome, and, with few other customers there, we recalled last year's pleasures with her. So in the space of a few hours we'd recovered tart, autobus, Metro, and Les Limours—there was almost no reason to stay in Paris longer.

Our way of traveling was based on having as few deadlines as possible. That meant choosing a hotel or inn in a town we expected to reach, but not committing ourselves by making a reservation. This was a trifle risky. Sometimes the hotel was not yet open for the summer, had disappeared (or we couldn't find it), or less frequently was full. We spent many a late evening searching for a place to lay our heads, and many more finding a place to eat. There is nothing like weariness and hunger for producing heated exchanges, but we found many memorable places to stay and many fabulous places to eat. It strikes me that

I may have portrayed this marriage as one of the "lived happily ever after" variety. It was not, and I suspect there really is no such thing. Real marriage takes constant work.

Perhaps responding to the harmony we both felt, Garret amazed me by suggesting we respond to an "apartment for sale" notice on a door in our friends' building. It *is a ground floor studio, and we are in the midst of plans, counter-plans, ifs, and buts about what to do and when, and where to go for advice, and why did the sign come down but the key remain in its hiding place?*

This is the last of Garret's diary, and I am sorry to leave it. The tone of Garret's writing suggests the whirlwind of ideas that surrounded us during the next week. We, of course, had no plans to move to Paris, but knew we would be coming back often. The plan was to rent the apartment to visitors at the Institute, especially those bringing family along. That was the practical side, worked out because the thrill of having a place of our own in France was delicious. I, for one, couldn't believe it. The tiny apartment was absolutely charming with two large casement windows opening onto the small courtyard set back from the busy street. Not only could we be very comfortable here, but our best friends in Paris lived five floors above us. It was, in a word, perfect. I'm afraid that the memory of all our sightseeing, including our second trip to Brittany, has been lost in the fog of sheer delight in setting up our "Paris apartment!" We were two children "playing house."

We bought the apartment in 1975 and kept it until 1982. I'm sure we both had some of the happiest days of our lives in that tiny pied-a-terre in Paris. We came often in the spring and learned to know Paris and much of France. My memories of the time are not very well organized, but some are still vivid.

Although we were not the first visitors to France to enjoy its food, we were among the most enthusiastic. In some ways our breakfasts in the apartment were the best of all. While I started the coffee Garret went to the bakery just a few doors away for a crunchy baguette or warm croissant, or to the pastry shop for a variety of goodies that included one I had never seen before, called pain au chocolat. Hidden inside a square of slightly sweet bread lies a generous piece of bitter chocolate—delicious.

Of course we did more than eat. Although we heard some fine music, there is one occasion I remember in particular, a recital held in Ste. Chapelle, the relatively small chapel whose very tall, narrow, red and blue stained-glass windows are unique. Although we sat on uncomfortable chairs crowded into the nave, the sound of flute and guitar together filled the air with magic.

Garret and Jacques, Berkeley, 1977. Garret had built the containers out of scrap for the move to Menorca.

A VERY SMALL CLOUD, 1975-1977

It was at this time that the search for larger and more complex interstellar molecules became intense. The dream was, I think, to find the presence of "benzene rings" with its implication as an essential precursor of life. I must say it seemed to me rather fanciful (and "fanciful" I usually avoided.) I found that I did not understand the complexities of molecular structure, and (worse) did not care. Still worse, I realized in a discussion with a student that I was pretending to know something that I didn't. It was a shock. Intellectual dishonesty is obviously bad in any situation, but in a scientific endeavor it is fatal.

My solution to my scientific disenchantment was to find a project that I might be able to do, but one that was so new to me that my colleagues would know I needed to learn from them. Again I was lucky. A group of astronomers from Caltech wanted to use their 130 foot antenna in the Owens Valley together with our 85 foot dish in Hat Creek to observe quasars at 20 cm wavelength. The observations would be made using the new technique of very long baseline interferometry (VLBI), because it provided far greater resolution than any other technique. The "magic" of this method is that in one way the instrument formed by the two antennas acts like an instrument the size of the distance between the two observatories, in this case about 300 miles. The size of its beamwidth approximates that of an antenna with such a huge diameter, resulting here in a resolution on the sky of less than 0.1" of arc (for comparison that is 1/18000 of the moon's diameter.) Of course the amount of radio radiation picked up by the instrument is limited by the total area of the two antennas—one does not quite get something for nothing.

Linking the two systems together to form a single instrument leads to great complexity both in the observations and their reduction. The primary requirement is that the two sites operate with time standards that are as close to identical as possible. Data is accumulated very rapidly and is stored on magnetic tape. The use of two-inch wide tape reduced the number of reels required to record it all. Sources are observed throughout the time that they lie above the horizon of both observatories, thus requiring a team of observers at each of them.

As we were planning for the observing time I made a bargain with the Caltech team. We would help with their observations if they would help us make our own. Since their chosen wavelength was so close to that of the hydrogen line, my idea was to use the high resolution to observe interstellar neutral hydrogen. No observations of the gas at such high resolution had ever been attempted, largely because no one expected such small scale features in the neutral gas. I saw no harm in trying, but did not realize how much study of a spectral line would complicate matters compared to continuum studies, although I should have.

"Continuum" sources are of many kinds but they share the characteristic of emitting radiation over a wide (continuous) range of frequencies. On the other hand, radiation arising from "clouds" of atoms (H) or molecules (OH) covers only a small range of frequencies, and much of the value of studying them lies in the fine detail within that range. Dealing with frequency as an additional variable meant further demands on the system both in observing and handling the data. For example, each receiver tuned to receive hydrogen used 100 separate channels, each isolating a narrow band of frequencies, allowing determination of the shape of the line profile, but multiplying the data flow needed for continuum sources by 100!

In the first observing run in November 1973 the frequency resolution was 10 KHz (2 km/sec), but that proved to be inadequate. So we tried again in July 1974 with 5 KHz (1 km/sec) channels, and that did the trick. After each of these observing runs I took the data to the National Radio Astronomy Observatory in Charlottesville, Virginia, to put it through the only existing "processor." This device, to put it delicately, was still under development, but provided the first step in the lengthy process of converting raw data into meaningful results. Also, it was here that the crucial question "Did the system work?" was answered. It did, but only after some very tense hours. This processor still required constant attention from its resident engineers, and from me, active cheerleading that included running up and down stairs (for what purpose I now don't remember).

My idea in this program was to determine whether small clouds exist in the interstellar gas—much smaller than any known. The best chance of finding these clouds was to observe a background source shining through hydrogen gas lying along the line of sight. The source should be made up of distinct and closely spaced components so that if one component shows the presence of a hydrogen cloud while the adjacent one does not, one can deduce that the cloud is smaller than the separation of components. I tried several candidates, but only the quasar 3C147 yielded positive results. It is made up of several small components, the major ones 0.16" apart and therefore resolved by our instrument, that is, distinguished as separate sources.

The known hydrogen-line absorption spectrum in the direction of 3C147 showed two clouds, at velocities of 0 and -8 km/s. Both these clouds appeared in our high-resolution observations, but there was a significant difference between the two. The 8 km/s cloud covered the whole source, while the zero velocity cloud covered one of the features within 3C147 but not the other 0.16" away. We may, of course, have been seeing the edge of a large feature that happened to lie between the two sources. (This seemed unlikely, but until more sources could be observed remained a possibility.) The alternative, that we were seeing a very small cloud having an angular size of only about 0.1" of arc, was the interpretation I explored.

In order to deduce the nature of this cloud in spite of the limitations of the observations, I had to make several (I hoped reasonable) assumptions. I found the linear diameter to be at most 3×10^{-4} pc or 60 AU (AU = astronomical unit = the distance from Earth to the Sun)!

The last paragraph in the paper on this research[43] describes the surprise best. "The cloud described here is smaller, by several hundred times, than any neutral hydrogen cloud previously observed; its size and density $[10^5$ cm$^{-3}]$ are more similar to those associated with dense molecular clouds. Speculations on the origin of such clouds, their place in the interstellar medium, and their influence on star formation depend critically on how large a fraction of the interstellar gas exists in this form."

The paper was published in June 1976, and immediately afterwards I began planning for further observations. This time we were able to use three antennas as our interferometer: Hat Creek and Owens Valley in California and the National Radio Astronomy Observatory's 140 foot telescope in Green Bank, West Virginia. This latter of course added a 3000 mile baseline. Scheduling the three antennas took some time, but the observations were made in early 1977. By now a new processor was operating at Caltech and it was there I scheduled time for examining our new material. Unfortunately, by the time I had finished there the date for my early retirement was imminent (more about that later.) I therefore had to leave the material with a colleague for final reduction. Still more unfortunately he never did anything with it.

That however was not the end of the story. Many years later, 13 in fact, I heard from my old friend and colleague, Miller Goss, that he (and collaborators) were able to detect clouds in the 25 AU range. They had observed again the neutral hydrogen absorption in front of 3C147 with three European VLBI antennas. They essentially verified our conclusions and in fact extended them to include two other sources, 3C138 and 3C380[44]. Then in the mid-1990s the National Radio Astronomy Observatory constructed the Very Long Baseline Array, ten antennas, located from Hawaii to the U.S. Virgin Islands, intended for high-resolution observations. The VLBA made mapping the very small clouds in great detail possible—a possibility beyond imagining when I first detected the cloud. Small-scale neutral hydrogen clouds have been observed using a variety of methods in the past 30 years(!)[45], suggesting that they are common throughout the galaxy. (In the diffuse molecular gas, in particular H_2CO, structures of this size and density have now also been found.) In May 2006 a colloquium on small ionized and neutral structures in the interstellar medium will be held in Socorro, NM. How I wish I could go! Explaining the presence of these very dense, small condensations in the interstellar gas remains a problem. One possibility proposed is that we are seeing not spherical clouds but a cross-section of filaments, but there is no direct evidence to support the idea. The model reminds me that Dr. Minkowski envisioned the interstellar medium as resembling a glass of iced coffee as the cream poured in.

ASTRONOMY, 1977

By 1977 I had been working in astronomy in one way or another for 30 years, and it was time I thought about all the changes those years had brought. I had chosen astronomy for a complex set of reasons, among them my feeling that science held a sort of security for me. In particular the physical sciences, so-called hard science, seemed to me to be based on a clear, precise foundation, one that might be difficult to understand but never uncertain. I thought that I could depend on my intellect, but that I could not depend on other people. I also knew that although much of that was my fault, I did not know how to change it. I remember very well being told that the way to be popular was to hide "how smart you are," but I neither knew how nor wanted to.

Like many young people I wanted to do something that mattered, something that would last. It soon became clear that my high-flown ambition would require not only very hard work but also a measure of luck. I found also that it would make my connecting with other people still more difficult—especially with women. If I had chosen something in the humanities, history or art or music, it would undoubtedly have been easier. For reasons that I still cannot fathom anyone who chooses science is thought to be somehow smarter, and all my protests to the contrary don't seem to make any difference. Surely the attitude must come in part from the unimaginative way science is taught in the early grades, but how to improve the method is quite beyond me.

That is not to say that astronomy provides an easy life. Acquiring the background in physics and mathematics is hard, both from the point of view of the struggle to understand and the constant challenge to one's confidence. Actually working in observational astronomy presents other problems, probably not the ones an outsider supposes. Imagine that you have an idea for a project and that you embark on the often slow and intricate process of gathering and interpreting data, enlisting the help of a skilled staff. It is vital, of course, that you carry out the project with absolute integrity, and without emotion, although in order to invest the effort in the first place you need to believe that the project is worth doing. An astronomer, or any scientist, fights a daily battle between emotion and discipline, and the job cannot be done without both.

On the other hand, I have found in astronomy a career always satisfying and occasionally thrilling. One persists through times of routine, demanding hours with the possibility of an extraordinary reward. Make no mistake; the approval of colleagues, especially those not familiar with your work, is wonderful, but it does not hold a candle to the joy in realizing that you are seeing something for the first time. In my experience there are two ways in which real discoveries are made: stumbling on something totally unexpected while looking at something else, and searching for something because you think it might be there. In my own work I found one of each.

The first was in the study of the OH molecule in the interstellar gas. Harold Weaver, David Williams, and I were all astonished at the strange behavior shown in our observations. Every new record seemed to contradict our assumptions. For me there was a special moment that occurred because I was in charge of collecting, organizing, and compiling the material sent from the observatory at Hat Creek. Because all the signals are weak, we needed to add together many days of observation of each source. As I was preparing to combine data obtained in July 1965 with that obtained in October, I realized with a shock that the two sets were different from one another, too different to combine. After scrambling through the records to determine whether they were indeed properly recorded and from the same source in the sky, I knew that I had in front of me irrefutable evidence that the interstellar gas changes in an unbelievably short time, a few months.

It was a delicious moment! However, I very nearly let my excitement lead me astray. I immediately set out to see if there were shorter term variations and found some changes over a few weeks. So why not days or hours? It looked to me as if there were some very short period changes, and only the advice of Harold Weaver led me to re-examine the validity of my conclusions. I had, it seems, let my excitement run away with me.

The second discovery occurred in quite a different way. Because a group of astronomers from Caltech had proposed to use our antenna and theirs as an interferometer at a frequency quite near that of neutral hydrogen, I had the opportunity to test for the first time my idea that clouds exist in the interstellar gas much smaller than any so far seen. This time the thrill of discovery was by no means immediate. It took long hours of observing and even more in processing the data before I knew I had been right. There was, however, the final moment when I knew that the data would prove it. There ain't, as they say, nothin' like it.

There was another difference in this project. In the case of OH, I faced reasonable skepticism that I was able to overcome because parts of the observed spectrum stayed the same while others varied. In the case of this unexpected, very small hydrogen cloud I encountered indifference. Although I left valuable information behind, no one bothered to examine it, and it was only 13 years later, when Miller and his colleagues wanted to see if they could verify my results with more modern techniques and higher sensitivity using the big antennas in Europe, that the observation was confirmed and extended. Without that confirmation the observation may just as well never have been done.

For many years now I had no longer needed astronomy as a source of what one might call psychological security; I had found Garret. He offered not only security but a life of discovery of another sort, of exploring the world and learning to reach the people in it. He was wonderfully talented at both. In early 1977 I learned that I could retire from the University that year when I was 51 years old with my pension to begin at 65. My health was not a major issue in the decision to leave astronomy, but I knew it could interfere in the now necessary extensive travel to other observatories.

Since Garret was already retired and we wanted to leave Berkeley, we decided to try living abroad and spent some months "throwing darts at maps" to decide where. We narrowed things a bit by focusing on islands (influenced by my love of Nantucket) and then on islands near Europe. The Spanish Balearic Islands in the Mediterranean seemed to fill the bill, and in the spring we journeyed there to choose which of the three, Mallorca, Menorca, or Ibiza.

1977-1981

MENORCA

That spring of 1977 we found the choice to be easy. Within just a few days we found Mallorca too full of tourists, Ibiza too hippie by half, and Menorca just right. Our first impression, of Menorca's airport, was remarkable in that there seemed to be a relaxed, unhurried atmosphere, suggesting that Menorca might be the place we were looking for. And then the quality of the light, the purity of the air, and the presence everywhere of the splendid beauty of the sea contributed to my feeling of a place unlike any I had ever known. It was only after living there that we could fully appreciate that this was truly a place apart.

At first we stayed in a house for rent in the off-season. It all seemed quite odd because there was so little of the things that normally filled our home: pictures, the "bears," (our affectionate name for the beautiful crystal sculpture of two polar bears swimming in an arctic sea) and the countless small things we had gathered. But there was a beautiful beach with fine, white sand and the crystal clear water of the Mediterranean. The houses arranged on winding streets along the hillside made a handsome picture with their gleaming white stone walls and red tile roofs.

Finally, we were able to buy the house that became the center of our stay. There were actually two buildings joined by a waist-high white stone wall with a wooden gate unlike any I had seen. Vertical pieces of wood four inches wide were held together by two curving pieces that looked like branches of a tree, all weath-ered to a soft gray. (We found that they were common throughout the island.) As we went through the gate, our excitement barely contained, we found on the right a building made of white stone slabs and a red tile roof. The walls were about a foot thick and very rough on the surface, and about 100 years old. A 4-foot high rough stone wall about 20 feet in front of the house formed a secluded patio (that we later covered with brick.) To the left of the house there was another wall with an opening that led to a raised area, an obvious place for a garden. Our first impression was that we were a long way from Berkeley, but not so far from Bodega.

The other old building had the remnants of an entrada that ended in a tiny room used, we were told, as a chicken coop. It was in this lofty spot that I spent many hours working at my potter's wheel. My chicken coop was a perfect studio, big enough for the paraphernalia of wheel, drying shelves, clay, and glazes. Beyond the patio our land extended a bit more than an acre, all of it covered either with trees or cactus. I made many charcoal drawings of parts of the yard, and they are (for me) better than any photograph for recalling the time. I especially like the ones of the cactus known as prickly pear, because the large, succulent leaves suggest something ancient, even prehistoric, while the delicate yellow flowers speak of spring and youth.

As soon as we were settled I became a student of a local, world class potter. Werner Bernard dug the clay, found the chemicals for glazes, and persuaded me to buy an electric potter's wheel because I could not spin the heavy cement disk of my wheel fast enough. His studio was like no other. It was a separate building down a long driveway guarded by a flock of geese—well, at least three. I had to brave their angry squawks and snapping beaks coming in and especially going out (not usually a digni-fied process.) Since the building had no doors they were free to come into the studio (less belligerently) where they were joined by various ducks and once by a small goat. In the winter it grew so cold in there that our fingers were numb from the cold water, not an ideal condition for feeling the clay on the wheel. Bernard was entirely unsympathetic, as he was in general. I found that his work set a high standard for me and my fellow students but Bernard considered himself a fine artist with little tolerance for mere mortals. I really did try very hard and found his sharp comments sometimes wounding. I hid my feelings pretty successfully, except on one occasion. I had what I thought was a great idea of building a medieval castle out of slabs of clay and some thrown pieces like the crenellated towers. For once I put up a spirited defense of my creation.

Bernard was right in his overall judgment of my ability to "throw pots" but neither he nor I knew why I was not progressing. I now believe that part of the problem lay in the insensitivity of my hands caused by MS (a comfort to my wounded pride.)

Our tiny "estate" was indeed a peaceful and remote one. I don't think I was aware of it at the time, but there was a remarkable absence of noise: virtually no traffic noise both because there were not a lot of cars on the road and because the maximum speed limit was 35 miles an hour. Of course, on our little dirt road with only three houses and two of them rarely occupied there was none. Noise from airplanes, all of them small, was heard at most a couple of times a day. There was no telephone to ring, although not by choice. We discovered it would take years and too much money to bring a line to us. And no beeping from microwave, pager, back-up warning signal, or computer. Only the occasional before-dawn song of a nightingale and Jacques' occasional barking at imaginary dragons and his monthly baying at the full moon (honest) broke the silence. It was not lonely, just quiet.

Unfortunately after just a few months of exploring I began to feel truly exhausted after even a short outing, because walking no longer came to me naturally. I had to think how to put one foot in front of another and lost some assurance in my balance. About the only thing that I could not do, however, was spend the morning at the market examining all the wonderful fresh goods. Garret did that part of the shopping for us. One summer we went to London, and it was on that trip that I was first persuaded to try a wheelchair and I had my first experience at being "handicapped." With Garret pushing me it was actually fun to ride along and look around freely with no requirement to watch my step. It was occasionally unnerving to discover that I was virtually invisible. At a counter in Harrod's where I was trying to choose a scarf, the sales lady looked at Garret over my head and said, "May I help you, sir?" My reply, "Speak to me, please," startled the clerk, but was entirely in line with my determination not to be a victim. And then there was the problem of navigating narrow aisles and avoiding unwary pedestrians. Although it was inconvenient, the chair freed me from the occasional overwhelming weariness that overtook me. With some reluctance (from me) on our return home we bought a wheelchair for just such times.

One English couple who owned the house just across from ours came from London for the summer and several times during the winter. Because we saw them often and they noticed my trouble in walking, I told them of my MS. It seems they had a friend who had a remedy for MS: a gluten-free diet. This was the first time I had come upon a "cure," and we decided to try it. Avoiding all products containing wheat posed quite a challenge in this community without health food stores or large supermarkets, but Garret with his usual energy and determination met the challenge and cheerfully stuck to the diet with me. Of course it had no effect, and the experience left me wary.

After about a year we gave up on the diet as a "cure" when I continued to have trouble walking and could not seem to get comfortable sitting either. Our neighbors just across the lane put us in touch with his brother, Kike, who was a doctor. Kike said that the steroid, prednisone, had shown positive results for the symptoms of MS and that I should try it. Perhaps this was the answer. What followed was a period of about 18 months during which Garret often tried to find Kike, usually unsuccessfully, so that he could advise me about the use of the drug. Fortunately, or so we thought, we could continue to get the drug without further need for a prescription.

Then as always I found that thinking about something else was the most effective cure. I continued with my pottery until one day Bernard said in his typical acerbic way, "You know what's wrong with you? You don't really look at things—when you think about a tree you see a lollipop shape. You should try drawing. That will make you really look." And he was right (much as I hated to agree). To prove his point he took the time to paint the scene behind his studio while I watched. After I tried my hand at painting myself, it was clear that I enjoyed painting, and that I would benefit from some real instruction. Again I was very fortunate in finding a real artist who was willing to give lessons to a beginner. Actually Wim Blom, originally a South African, was already a friend. We had bought his painting of houses in San Luis, and it still hangs on my wall. Garret liked my charcoal sketches of our house and yard so much that I made a great number of them that I now treasure.

There were times when we simply had fun. We discovered a small cala (a sort of cove) where a few boats were anchored. At the friendly small cafe on the beach we found the perfect sailboat for sale. It was a sloop about 15 feet long equipped with a pair of oars for windless times and a centerboard that made it possible to sail right up to the beach. Just outside the sheltered cala was more open water leading to a sandy beach one could reach only by boat. Sailing around the small island just offshore was sometimes a challenge because of the shifting winds, but after San Francisco Bay it was tame indeed. It was a joy to sail again, particularly because I could still hold up my end as first mate.

Since prednisone did not seem to help I decided to stop taking it. At about the same time someone knew of a doctor, actually a psychiatrist, who had had some success in treating MS. In for a penny, in for a pound: I went to see him. His solution was the use of vitamins, especially B12. I was to have an injection in my hip that Garret could administer every other day. Neither of us had any idea what this would mean. The effect, as described by a friend, is quite like being kicked by a mule. Hard as I tried I could not stop crying out each time. I can only guess the effect on my private "nurse."

One December evening our English neighbors told us that they were planning a trip to the United States and wanted our guidance about what places to visit. We thought of historic places because of their interest in antiques, of beautiful scenery rather than cities, and cool, pleasant summer weather. As Garret and I talked, it became obvious to both of us that New England was the place. In fact, we were, both of us, suddenly and unexpectedly homesick. It was probably that evening or, at the latest the next morning, that we decided to go home. We began immediately to plan a brief trip in January to Vermont, first of all to determine whether we really wanted to do this, and then to look for a house.

I continued working with Wim until shortly before we left Menorca. Toward the end I was often not feeling well enough to paint, particularly frustrating because we were working on a scene I especially wanted to record. It has a stone wall and gate and a stand of beautiful cypresses. I asked Wim if he would consider painting it for me, but he said he never accepted a commission for painting a specific subject. The day we left Menorca we were surprised at the airport by a large group of our friends, including Wim who came bearing a gift: a fine oil painting of my cypresses. It also hangs on my wall, bringing back a special memory of Menorca, the quality and serenity of its light, and of course the generosity of a friend.

1981 – 1998

VERMONT

ABIGAIL'S HOUSE, 1981

Our trip to Vermont in January 1981 was a success beyond our expectations. The whole week was frigid but the cold, clear air and icy sunshine illuminated a landscape transformed by a cover of unblemished snow. We had made the trip in winter to sample the worst of New England weather, but were instead overcome by the pure beauty of a place where there are "more trees than people."

Best of all we found a remarkable house with a rich history of which I learned more through the very small branch library in "downtown" North Thetford. I should say that in addition "downtown" consisted of a general store, a tiny post office, and a church. The house had been built in 1796 and I found a picture of its mistress, Abigail Horsford. She was married in 1796 at 20 years old, bore 12 children, and died at the ripe old age of 82. There is a story that once when the men of the village were away, probably hunting, Abigail learned that warlike Indians were approaching. She rounded up the women and children and managed to get them across the river to safety. This was one resourceful woman! I always felt that we did not own the house but cared for it for her and all the others who had followed. How she and Joseph raised 12 children in that small house with no modern insulation or sophisticated heating remains a constant wonder. I thought of her often on cold winter nights when it took the oil furnace and a fancy wood stove to keep the house warm.

In many ways the surroundings of our house were unchanged from Abigail's day. Far to the East we looked at distant mountains giving us a sort of birds-eye view of the pattern of change from green to flame to brown and then to white, and to the west, hillsides close enough to see the individual trees that make up such a pattern. And on our own land: grass that would never be a lawn, and great maple trees 60 to 70 feet high. It was all simply beautiful.

Abigail's House. Acrylic by Nan Dieter Conklin.

PAIN, 1982

We lived in this wonderful house for 17 years, but for much of the time a new element had entered our lives—pain. It began with persistent pain in my upper left arm. Garret began driving me three times a week to the hospital where various therapists first heated and then cooled my shoulder in preparation for their fiendish exercises. At home he suspended a series of pulleys and ropes from one of the beams in the living room in order for me to do my own exercises. It was the first of many such inventions.

It did not take long for the doctor to find the source of the trouble. It was transferred pain originating in my adrenal glands that naturally produce cortisol as well as adrenaline but had ceased working altogether. The plan was to begin taking cortisone again in carefully regulated doses with the hope of reviving the natural function. Untreated it could be life-threatening, and was clearly the result of my extended use of prednisone.

My memory of the time that followed is a bit cloudy but I know that I spent the better part of a year in bed. About halfway through the time the tests indicated that my system was responding, but at just that time new symptoms developed. There was a persistent pain in my abdomen obviously connected to a malfunctioning colon. The pain was now constant, and there seemed to be no solution. For the few seconds that it took for me to come fully awake in the morning I felt no pain at all, but then it hit me and remained an almost tangible presence until I slept again. The experience changed my outlook on life and also changed Garret's and my relationship. It must have been terrible for him to be unable to "fix it," although he tried in every way he could. I came to depend upon him for everything, and when he finally asked "What happened to the woman I married?" I realized I must do something.

Since there seemed to be no cure for the pain itself, I needed to find a way to live with it. I knew that the trick was to find a way to think of something else. First I tried the biofeedback techniques available at the hospital and found them not only helpful but also interesting. Probably the most important concept I learned there was that there are two aspects to pain, one, the physical fact and two, my reaction to it. The first I had no control over, the second I did. What I needed to do was relax, but since there is no switch to throw for overall relaxing, I needed to concentrate on one group of muscles at a time. What I found interesting was the way I could tell that I was being successful —the feedback. I held between two fingers a very small thermometer that measured the temperature of my skin, between 70 and 80 degrees: falling when I relaxed and rising when I tensed again. Occasionally I managed self-hypnosis, but usually I was able to meditate deeply enough to have a little time at peace.

I also found several ways within my limitations to keep in touch with the world. The Library of Congress books on tape for the blind and handicapped provided me with hours of stimulating books. The enormous selection of books and the non-intrusive, talented readers made listening a new, rewarding alternative. And then I rediscovered baseball, forgotten since my youth, on television from Wrigley Field in Chicago. After some instruction in the finer points of the game Garret watched the games with me and we became rabid Cubs fans.

To help Garret take care of me and the house we found a young woman who endeared herself to me on her first visit. She came with a handful of new-mown hay from the pasture across the road. The scent of the outside world was a priceless gift.

I was spending more time downstairs now, and we bought a stair-glide to make it easier. The track for the mechanism went straight down along the stairs to the landing two steps above the main floor, and for a while that was all right. When I could no longer climb those two steps, Garret made his most ingenious contraption. It was made of a double pulley arrangement to hold a swing just above the bottom of the stairs. I stood and turned to sit on the seat; he pulled me up to the level of the stair-glide where I twisted around to sit—and hence up the stairs. Pure Garret!

Vermont Winter. Watercolor by Nan Dieter Conklin.

WINTER – AND PENNY

Meanwhile we came to learn about the life of this rural community. Probably most important was the rhythm of the seasons. Winter in Vermont is surpassingly beautiful, with its magical transformation of the landscape into a graceful, pure, and, in a way, abstract world that muffles all sounds but the sharp crack of shattering ice. As we looked out our windows onto the front yard on a bitterly cold night, the snow piled high and glittering with ice crystals, and the moon casting long, eerie, shadows of our great maples, we felt transported to Narnia (except here there was a Christmas.)

At the end of such a winter in 1983 Penny Adams came to help with housekeeping, cooking, and caring for me, and left 13 years later one of my dearest friends. She was born the year I graduated from college, but there was nothing mother-daughter about our relationship. She was far too independent for that. She was also fiercely unsentimental, in fact, showed her feelings very little and will be embarrassed at my writing about her at all. She came faithfully five days a week at 8 a.m. but could not come earlier because she went first to fix her grandmother's breakfast. When I learned how much Penny hated getting up early, I realized how much that was a labor of love.

Penny helped me accept my physical dependence by her attitude in doing things for me. It was all quite matter-of-fact, not a bit condescending, and nothing to make a fuss about. I had found perhaps for the first time in my life a real woman friend. We talked of many things, some "girl talk," books, movies and TV shows. My description makes it sound rather superficial but the circumstances made it otherwise. She knew all about my struggle with pain and the strain it put on our marriage.

Penny made clothes for me from patterns and fabric that I chose. We did a bit of gardening, but most of all Penny cooked, often at my direction. It was really the best of both worlds for me, because I could experiment with recipes, learn new ones and new combinations all without having to do the tiresome chopping and cleaning up. It is indeed a tribute to our friendship that we never came to blows over cooking, even though I am sure Penny never took direction from anyone in her own kitchen. But we had fun.

SPRING

Winters are long in northern New England and one can easily be deceived by hints of spring. March often has storms with heavier snowfall than February, and in my new wisdom about Vermont weather I once predicted a blizzard on March 25th. I was the only one happy to see it come!

Spring usually comes in fits and starts—a slightly warmer, sunnier day, followed by a gray, cold rainy one. In the woods and along the roads clouds of pale green seem to hover over the willows and small, common trees blossom with tiny white flowers. Across our dirt road Mr. Palmer began preparing his pasture for the summer, and as I watched him on his tractor go around and around and around until the ground was turned over in patterns of dark brown earth, he waved to me with a smile. I remember how eagerly we spoke of these first signs that winter was indeed over.

Pain had become my constant companion. My physician tried all the diagnostic tools: CAT scan, MRI, colonoscopy, and no doubt some I have forgotten. The pain clinic at the hospital tried a nerve-block, but warned me that it might not last. Garret stood beside me and held my hand, as he so often did, while a doctor gave me the injection. After just a moment the pain was gone! It was a brilliant ray of sunshine. For just about 30 seconds I was free, but the return of the pain unchanged was a crushing blow to us both.

Most of the time I sat in a recliner with a heating pad on my abdomen, but was able to sit up for short periods. It was then that a friend loaned me an old computer, one that operated on the MS-DOS system with a black and white monitor, but at the time (mid-1980s) a magical device. I had, of course, worked with computers at Berkeley, but much had happened since then, and this was my introduction to the new world. One of the things I learned to do was to use the spreadsheet program to keep track of our investments. The major work was done by John Kautz, our trust manager, and Garret, but record-keeping on the computer was so easy that I enjoyed it.

It was about this time, I think, that I tried another approach to controlling the pain: acupuncture. (By the way my memory for times and details is clouded by pain and the medication to relieve it.) My foray into "alternative medicine" was interesting and instructive. Several times a week we went to the hour-long sessions. Garret drove and then waited for me, over and over again, all without the slightest suggestion of impatience. A considerable part of the treatment required lying in a very quiet room with meditative music, all intended for complete relax-ation. Putting the needles in didn't hurt at all, but the slightest movement afterwards caused a sharp, odd pain. It was all very interesting and helpful while I was there but led to no overall improvement.

During the course of the sessions the practitioner sang the praises of a macrobiotic diet and its value in overall health. The idea appealed to Garret and I thought, "What harm would it do?" Unfortunately it can do harm if it is not fully understood. We tried tofu and miso in every form you can imagine until my digestive system rebelled and I began to lose weight. It was only when I noticed my bones were complaining that I discov-ered my weight—75 pounds! That sent me to the hospital where they started a feeding program with a tube down my throat. I came home with the tube in place and a machine that introduced liquid food into my stomach at regular intervals overnight. I remember that it made little thumps all night long. Each morning Garret held me in his arms as he stepped on the scale to check our progress. When he could no longer lift me easily, the crisis was over.

SUMMER

We spent many summer afternoons in the yard, Garret preparing wood for the winter and I admiring his strength and vitality. No one really believed that he was in his 70s. Summer was a time for good food: sweet corn picked only hours before eating; tomatoes warmed by the sun, served with fresh crisp lettuce; strawberries and blackberries for eating and making jam. For our dogs it was the perfect season because we were out of doors to throw tennis balls and make attempts at training. We had a succession of black standard poodles beginning with Jacques. As he was growing older we found him a companion puppy named Tory, who was a little too energetic for our elder states- man. Then later, to keep Tory company, we got Rebel, followed by Shadow and Jenny. They all loved the freedom to roam and run, and I loved watching them.

Garret found opportunities to volunteer again and was always happy doing so. The hospital at Dartmouth offered him a chance to be part of a new system called Lifeline. It is a familiar service now but it was all new then and full of problems—just the sort of challenge for my Garret. Although I knew that one of the benefits of Lifeline is the peace of mind it gives to a care- giver when he is away, I stubbornly insisted that I didn't need it, that I could always get to the telephone for help. As they say, "Pride goeth before a fall." One afternoon while Garret was away I slipped off my chair onto the floor, not a bit hurt, but unable to get up. When Garret came home I greeted him meekly with "You win."

Our days passed at the pace of rural life, dominated by the season, and mostly spent alone. I can scarcely imagine how difficult this time must have been for Garret. He knew quite well the pain I was enduring but instead of hovering with sympathy he chose to help my life go on in spite of it.

Occasionally he had to get away for a few days for respite but I know that the trips were not very successful because I was not there. For both of us time together was invariably better than time apart. I remember that we were sitting at breakfast one morning talking about the news or books we had just read or any of a thousand other things when Betty Dugdale (a second faithful caregiver) said, "I don't believe you two. Most couples married as long as you have nothing much to talk about, but you always do."

There were times when Garret had in my judgment too many glasses of beer, and I was good deal less tolerant of it than I might have been. He was never even close to being drunk, but it frightened me, and one day I realized why. In frustration I said to him, "You are not really here. There is a veil in front of your eyes that shuts me out. We are wasting precious time." I had no idea how right I was.

AUTUMN

Autumn in Vermont is, most of all, a season of the spirit. "Leaf-peepers from the flatlands" see only the surface, splendid as that is. Although true Vermonters would scoff at my assessment, it is a time of melancholy as well as a time of wonder. It is as if the explosion of color punctuates the end of summer so dramatically that it forces one to face the inexorable coming of winter.

Best of all were the maples around our house. Their wide-spreading branches gave me the feeling of being suspended in a world of fluttering golden light. Some of the branches had leaves of a red for which there is no name, because it was made of light that changed with the slightest breeze. The first wind-storm sent a cascade of color to the ground below where the leaves piled in luminous drifts perfect for walking, with the unmistakable rustling sound of autumn. For a while the yard was covered with a glowing blanket that slowly faded to brown.

It was my job to find ways to widen my horizons. In 1987 (6 years after coming to Vermont) I sent letters to a dozen universities asking to audit courses by having a student tape record the lectures. Two schools replied positively, Cornell and Goucher, my alma mater. For the next couple of years I had a great time largely due to the interest and kindness of professors at each school. At Cornell I found several linguistics courses that appealed to me, especially since I didn't really know what linguistics meant, and at Goucher I chose music history and music appreciation. The professors did everything they could to make my scheme work, including managing the tapes and providing textbook and notes. I still have those notes.

Although I had some success at these distractions they did not always work. I was certainly anxious and depressed, especially after the doctor gave up and put me on morphine. I remember very clearly that I said to Penny, "I don't see the point in this. If I could end my life without hurting Garret I would do so." Her reply in her sternest voice was "You can't do that." She was right.

Garret and Jacques in Menorca.

HOPE, 1992

In early 1992 I met the first of my visiting nurses, Karen Gerrigan. Having a nurse come to a patient's home gives the experience quite a different quality, because the turf belongs not to the authoritative hospital, but to the patient. The burden is on the nurse not only to carry out her medical duties, but also to accept that she is a visitor and to act accordingly. The visits were social occasions that were precious to me in my isolation, particularly because all the nurses, and later on the therapists, were dedicated and interesting young people. Karen, the first, also changed my life forever.

By this time I had been on heavy doses of morphine for about a year, and she came to check on me about once a month. Then came a "fateful" day that seemed, at the time, quite ordinary. Karen suggested that I go to the hospital to see a friend of hers, a physician's assistant doing research in urology, whose help I could certainly use. The friend was Mary Ellen Kopening. What I found unusual was the intensity with which she listened to me. She was aware that I was in pain the whole time and in her direct way said "Well, that is clearly a larger problem. Are you game to try what I will propose?"

"Game?" I said. "I'm ready to try anything." In an attempt to dampen my expectations Mary Ellen warned that it would not be easy and might not work. Her idea was to treat the symptoms that could be treated and forget about the underlying cause, at least at first. She planned to treat the chronic constipation, and I remember vividly that she said, "Let's attack it from both ends!" And attack we did with massive doses of laxatives and various kinds of fierce enemas. Several months went by with some improvement but without much effect on the pain. Then in about eight or nine months I found that there were actually times without pain. My spirits soared.

Mary Ellen decided that occupational and physical therapists could be a help in regaining my strength and my mobility. From the physical therapist, John, I learned more than exercises. One day I was leaning back in a chair, and John said, "Now, lean forward." It's hard to remember now how hard it was to do so, but I kept trying to catch hold of something to pull myself forward. And trying, and trying, and trying again. Finally he said, "Stop, Nan. Stop and think of a different way." It was such a simple thing, but it has resonated with me ever since. I realized that this was the way I often approach a problem, certain of the way to solve it, and unwilling to realize that the way may be wrong.

My aim in the therapy was to stand again and use a walker. Again I kept trying and trying. Garret continued to hope until John brought him to see me struggle to stand with the walker. We both knew then that I would never walk again. I could not know what that would come to mean, but I was so thankful to be free of pain that it seemed a minor matter.

When I had been free of morphine for a while, I learned what it had been doing to me. Apparently there were major gaps in my memory, and times when I had made no sense whatever. It's hard to imagine what that might have meant to Garret, especially during the time when there seemed to be no end to it.

Gradually the intense pain receded altogether. I don't know why relieving my body of the strain on my digestive system had such an effect, but I do know that it greatly reduced my anxiety level. The complexity of the body-mind system probably makes the reason unknowable, but it hardly matters. Enduring the pain for such a long time had a profound effect. It left behind a person who has learned how much she depends on others, and not only for physical assistance, and who savors life and its opportunities with delight.

PAINTING, 1994

I wanted most of all to try painting again. I began by copying photographs of pictures that I loved—the cave paintings at Lascaux. Trying to do so required me to look very, very carefully at each scene and in the process I came to enjoy them even more. I made about a dozen paintings that still hang on my wall, reminding me of that magic 20 minutes we spent in the cave long ago. That is, in fact, the continuing value of my paintings. They take me back to times and places I want to remember in a way no photograph can.

During this time we found the dynamic of our marriage to be changing. I no longer was so dependent on Garret physically or emotionally, and was somewhat impatient when he made decisions for me. In fact, we sought the advice of a marriage counselor who, finding our disagreements surprisingly mild under the circumstances, said that she was sure we would soon straighten things out on our own. And, of course, we did. Then in February 1997 everything changed again. Garret was rushed to the hospital with a pain in his side. He and Betty Dugdale waited in the emergency room for hours until a nurse took his temperature and discovered a high fever. A burst appendix demanded immediate surgery, and all I could do was wait by the telephone. To my enormous relief the surgeon called to say all was well and that he felt it unlikely any infection would follow. What did follow were the lingering effects of the anesthetic.

They seemed to change Garret's invariably stoic response to pain and illness (except for a descent into abject misery with the onset of a head cold.) He began to complain more and more about the pain in his back and hips that had troubled him for some time. The doctors at the pain clinic decided that the answer was to treat the pain with narcotics of increasing potency. They did not seem to help much and, in addition, caused terrifying psychological symptoms. To call them terrifying is not an exaggeration. One afternoon in early July Garret was working in the yard, and I opened the front door to go out on our little porch to be with him. When I turned to look to my right, I could not believe my eyes because my beautiful garden of peonies lay in ruins. It was like a physical blow to my chest. When I weakly said, "Why?" Garret's response was, "We are going to have the house painted and I needed to clear the way for the painter." All this may seem high drama for so small an event, but my Garret would never have cut down the beautiful plants that meant so much to me.

I needed to make a decision, and I must do it alone. Garret's cloud of confusion showed no sign of lifting, and our children were urging us to move both closer to a city and closer to them. It was hard to accept that it was no longer enough to have one another. The choice in the end was Seattle because Amy was there. Our doctor told me to observe Garret's condition and if it had not improved by late fall to consult a neurologist.

1998 -

SEATTLE

The move was a nightmare. We had lived in our farmhouse for 17 years and now I needed to go through everything we had accumulated to choose what to keep. I gave away many things, books to the library, plants to friends. And then there were the dogs, Shadow and Jenny, who were bewildered by all the activity, and presented some problem in traveling by air. The cross country trip finally ended at our rented house in Seattle where there was so much to do, all of it alarmingly expensive. I needed to find a family doctor, to buy the small dumpster used for trash collection, to set up an account with the power company, to arrange with the water utility for fresh water and wastewater collection, to start telephone services, to decipher the inscrutable heating-cooling system, to apologize to neighbors for the dogs' barking, to take down the new bird feeder because I was told it attracted rats, and all of this before our belongings and our car had arrived. (Just listing these things reminds me of the nearly intolerable anxiety of those days and the crushing weariness I felt.) Through it all Garret could be no help, and I missed him terribly. For him the move was simply something to live through, and I can only hope that he was unaware of how much I needed him. In retrospect I'm not sure how I did it.

The time came for me to find a neurologist for Garret. At the first visit he carried out a simple test that consists of a series of questions designed to evaluate the patient's awareness of his surroundings. For example, what month is it, where are you, who is president, draw a clock face with numbers on it and indicate a time, etc. Garret's replies showed me the depths of his confusion. We made an appointment for an MRI in a couple of weeks, and a couple of weeks after that we saw the doctor again. This time he spoke mostly to me alone. He said, "In this kind of dementia ..." and then stopped because he had seen the look of alarm on my face. "It's a term commonly used in the medical profession. Anyway, the purpose of the MRI is to show the cause of the dementia, whether it is due to a series of small strokes or to early-stage Alzheimer's. In Garret's case it is Alzheimer's." In my despair I could not speak. In a few moments he asked, "Where are you living?" When I told him he asked me another question, "Do you want to die when your husband does? If not, you must move to a facility where you can get help or you will kill yourself."

NORTHSHORE HOUSE, April 1999-October 2003

There really was no choice. We clearly needed help, and an assisted-living facility seemed to be the answer. Living in such a place, however, is not without its emotional as well as financial cost. Perhaps the greatest was that we could not take Shadow and Jenny, but knowing that they would be happy with one of Garret's daughters on her 20 acres in Northern California helped (a little). I found the further loss of independence difficult, particularly because my time was not my own. My rising in the morning, my days to shower, my mealtimes, and many other things were not under my control anymore. Also I had to deal with many people every day: an ever-changing staff of aides, a management staff almost as unstable, and of course the other residents.

In return I got the help I must have, and Garret found a greater sense of security so that I could leave him for a few hours at a time. He was gradually forgetting how to do the simplest things, and I remember being angry that he could not even wash the dishes, followed by inevitable guilt. It is a pattern common to caregivers, but it doesn't really help to know that. However, in the Northshore Senior Center's writing group I found a friend. Although our backgrounds are quite different, Nancy Ray and I continue to learn how similar we are. Our friendship has lived through times that were close to unbearable for each of us, and has grown stronger for sharing them.

As time went by Garret receded from me a little each day. There was now a permanent veil between us so that what I saw in his eyes was a heartbreaking blankness. Most of the time he did not know what was happening to him, but I remember one day when he asked, "How can I get out of this?" I was stunned because I could neither lie to him nor tell him the truth. We shared an apartment for three years until May 2002 when he had to move to the secure dementia unit. I am grateful that when I came to visit him each day he continued to know me. In the middle of August our doctor told me that she felt he had no more than six months to live. I am so glad that I heard such news from a woman who knew what it would mean to me, and who at the same time knew how to help me face it.

Dr. Smith advised me to enter Garret into the Hospice program, and that same day arranged for me to meet with one of their representatives who could explain the program to me. That was Wednesday and the lady came on Saturday afternoon to tell me what they could do to help. Together we went to see Garret who was tossing restlessly on his bed in a way that alarmed me. Since there was nothing I could do, I went to dinner, and afterwards transferred, with the help of an aide, to my recliner. I was sitting there when at about 7 o'clock a nurse came breathlessly into the room to say, "You had better come. I think the end is near." My aide got me back into the wheelchair in record time, and I flew down to Garret's room scarcely breathing on the way. When I saw the change in him, I asked the nurse to call Nancy.

He was lying there so quietly, clearly withdrawing from the world around him. I took his hand and felt a thrill as he held mine in a gesture so familiar that I was flooded with memory. In a few moments I began talking to him, and even sang a little —"All Through the Night," and "Over the Rainbow." I knew he wouldn't mind this time my poor attempt at carrying a tune. Soon Nancy came and held my other hand in her quiet way. And then I became aware of the drama unfolding before me. I was in the presence of one of the great mysteries of life—its end. For Garret it was peaceful and I would guess welcome. And then it was over.

EPILOGUE, 2005

That was August 17th, 2002, and sometime in the blur of the weeks that followed I was given a large American flag in recognition of Garret's service in the Second World War. I decided to give it to Northshore House to hang on the tall flag pole at the entrance. I had my service of remembrance when we raised the flag a month later on the first anniversary of September 11th.

I have not shed a tear. My desolation is deeper than weeping. I have moved with Jenny, my quirky cat (old ladies, it seems, have the right idea), to a splendid retirement community, Brittany Park. Since I can no longer stand I need help in doing practical things: my nimble electric wheelchair allows me to get around with ease, and a hand-operated hydraulic lift makes possible easy transfers. Since my right leg no longer takes orders from me, I wear a brace to keep it upright.

My apartment faces due south, and that allows me to have an indoor garden where for the first time I am growing orchids. After many attempts at cultivating other plants as bonsai, I'm having some success with a ficus. (Under its arching branches is a tiny model of our Menorcan house.) I'm not at all sure that Garret would approve of my extravagance in having a 50 gallon saltwater reef aquarium, but he would love the tiny creatures. I'm also having fun with fine clothes, in some sense another palette for color and texture. (I quiet my conscience with savvy bidding on eBay.)

One more thing—

I have been troubled off and on with pressure sores caused by the brace. We have tried different solutions including soft sleep-boots, but sometimes the irritation is enough to keep me awake. One evening my aide, while helping me to bed, asked shyly,

"Do you mind if I pray over your foot?" I was touched both because she cared enough and because she knew I would not react with hostility, although certainly with skepticism. That was about two months ago and my foot has not hurt again. It was a perfect scientific experiment that left me knowing that something extraordinary had happened. The experience leads me to wonder—are there really Three Paths to Heaven's Gate?

Paris Apartment. Acrylic by Nan Dieter Conklin.

Endnotes

[1] Hepburn, N. and Hagen, J.P. 1952. "Solar Outbursts at 8.5mm Wavelength" Nature 170: 244.

[2] Ewen, H.I. and Purcell, E.M. 1951. "Radiation from Galactic Hydrogen at 1420 Mc/s" Nature 168, 356. Confirming papers: Muller, C.A. and Oort, J.H. 1951. "The Interstellar Hydrogen Line at 1420 Mc./sec, and an Estimate of Galactic Rotation" Nature 168: 357. See also the note by J.L. Pawsey following the paper by Muller and Oort. The Australian results were published more fully in 1952 by Christiansen and Hindman: Australian Journal of Scientific Research A5, 437.

[3] Hepburn, N.; Hagen, J. P.; McClain, E. F. 1954 "Detection of Discrete Radio Sources at 21 cm Wavelength" Proc. IRE, 42, 1811.

[4] Hagen, J. P.; McClain, E. F.; Hepburn, N. 1954. "Radio Discrete Sources and Galactic Absorption at 21 cm Wave Length" Astron. J., 59, 323.

[5] Hepburn, N. 1952. "A Photometric Study of the Solar Corona" Astrophys. J., 122, 445.

[6] Hagen, J. P.; McClain, E. F.; Hepburn, N. 1954. "Radio Discrete Sources and Galactic Absorption at 21 cm Wave Length" Astron. J., 59, 323.

[7] For a full account of Cecilia Payne-Gaposchkin's life see Cecilia Payne-Gaposchkin: an autobiography and other selections, edited by Katherine Haramundanis. Cambridge University Press, 1984 (1st ed.) and 1996 (2nd ed.). [Eds.]

[8] Heeschen, D.S. and Dieter, N.H. 1957. "Extragalactic 21 cm Line Studies" Proc. IRE, 46, 234.

[9] Dieter, N.H. 1958. "Neutral Hydrogen in M33" Astron J., 63, 49.

[10] Dieter, N.H. 1962. "Neutral Hydrogen in M33" Astron. J., 67, 270.

[11] Dieter, N.H. 1960. "Neutral Hydrogen in OB Associations" Astrophys. J., 132, 49.

[12] Murray, B.C.; Dieter, N. 1960. "Tangential Velocity Measurements – An Independent Approach to Geodesy" GRD Research Notes, no. 41.

[13] Dieter, N.H. 1962. "Neutral Hydrogen in M 101" Astron. J., 67, 317.

[14] Dieter, N.H. 1962. "Neutral Hydrogen in IC 342" Astron. J., 67, 313.

[15] Dieter, N.H. 1962. "A Search for HI in Centaurus A" Astron. J., 67, 222.

[16] Dieter, N.H. and Ewen, H.I. 1964. "Radio Observations of the Interstellar OH Line at 1667 Mc/s" Nature, 201, 279.

[17] Dieter, N.H. and Goss, W.M. 1966. "Recent Work on the Interstellar Medium" Rev. Mod. Phys., 38, 256.

[18] The 85 foot telescope at Hat Creek Observatory was dedicated on June 7, 1962. It collapsed in an ice storm on January 21, 1993. [Eds.]

[19] Weaver, H.F. and Williams, D.R.W. 1964. "OH Absorption Profile in the Direction of Sagittarius A" Nature, 201, 380.

[20] Weinreb, S.; Barrett, A.H.; Meeks, M.L.; Henry, J.C. 1963. "Radio Observations of OH in the Interstellar Medium" Nature, 200, 829.

[21] Dieter, N.H. and Ewen, H.I. 1964. op. cit.

[22] Hartmann, J. 1904. "Investigations on the Spectrum and Orbit of ä Orionis" Astrophys. J., 19, 268.

[23] See note 2 above.

[24] Rudolph Minkowski was born in Germany in 1895. His father was a physician, and his uncle, Hermann, was the mathematician reknowned for his idea of the space-time continuum. Rudolph Minkowski worked in both physics and observational astronomy at University of Hamburg, then came to the U.S. in 1935 to join his friend Walter Baade at Mt. Wilson Observatory. He studied spectra of novae, of supernovae and their remnants, and of planetary nebulae, and designed instruments, including Schmidt cameras, for spectographic work. He oversaw the National Geographic Society-Palomar Sky Survey of the northern sky in the 1950s. Together with Baade, he made optical identifications of many radio sources, including Cygnus A, and in 1960 Minkowski found in a galaxy what remained for many years the largest known redshift. He retired from Mt. Wilson in 1960, and then joined the staff at the Radio Astronomy Laboratory, University of California at Berkeley. He remained at Berkeley until his second retirement in 1965. He was a member of the National Academy of Sciences, and received the Bruce Medal in 1961. Minkowski died in 1976. [Eds.]

[25] Weaver, H.; Williams, D.R.W.; Dieter, N.H.; Lum, W.T. 1965. "Observations of a Strong Unidentified Microwave Line and of Emission from the OH Molecule." Nature, 208, 29. [Despite the fact that the authors were uncertain if they were seeing OH and thought there might be a new transition, whimsically called Mysterium, this paper is now considered to be the beginning of interstellar maser research. Using the 60 foot telescope at Harvard, Ellen Gunderman Hardeback had found the masers earlier, but did not publish the results. Eds.]

[26] Now time variations are universally accepted as being prominent. We even find variations on 20 minute time scales using VLBA data, e.g. Deshpande, Ramachandran and Goss, Astrophys. J., in press 2006. [Eds.]

[27] Weaver, H.; Dieter, N.H.; Williams, D.R.W. 1968. "Observations of OH Emission in W3, NGC 6334, W49, W51, W75, and ORI a" Astrophys. J. Suppl., 16, 219.

[28] Dieter, N.H. and Goss, W.M. 1966. op. cit.

[29] Dieter, N.H. 1967. "Observations of the Hydrogen Recombination Line 158α in Galactic H II Regions" Astrophys. J., 150, 435.

[30] Spinrad, H.; Sargent, W.L.W.; Oke, J.B.; Neugebauer, G.; Landau, R.; King, I.R.; Gunn, J.E.; Garmire, G.; Dieter, N.H. 1971. "Maffei 1: A New Massive Member of the Local Group?" Astrophys. J., 163, L25.

[31] If we had looked for hydrogen in M2 instead of M1, we would have found a nice detection. M1 is an elliptical galaxy which we now know to have very little interstellar hydrogen.

32 Heiles, C.; Habing, H. J. 1974. "An Almost Complete Survey of 21 cm Line Radiation for $|b| >= 10°$ I. Atlas of Contour Maps" Astron. Astrophys. Suppl. 14, 1.

33 Weaver, H.; Williams, D.R.W. 1973. "The Berkeley Low-Latitude Survey of Neutral Hydrogen Part I. Profiles" Astron. Astrophys. Suppl., 8, 1.

34 Dieter, N.H. 1971. "Berkeley Survey of High-Velocity Interstellar Neutral Hydrogen" Astron. Astrophys., 12, 59.

35 The author and editors remind the reader that the facilities and state of radio astronomy in the former Soviet Union have changed greatly since the 1973 events described in this book, and the book reflects the experiences of the author in a radically different research environment than that of the present time. [Eds]

36 Now called the Puschino Radio Observatory. Serpakov is the nearby large city. [Eds.]

37 Shklovsky describes his visit to Berkeley in his book Five Billion Vodka Bottles to the Moon: Tales of a Soviet Scientist. W.W. Norton, 1991. See p. 235 ff. [Eds.]

38 The RATAN-600 saw first light on July 12, 1974, and, in 2005, is still in use. [Eds.]

39 Snyder, L.E.; Buhl, D.; Zuckerman, B.; Palmer, P. 1969. "Microwave Detection of Interstellar Formaldehyde" Phys. Rev. Lett., 22, 679.

40 Dieter, N.H. 1973. "A Survey of Interstellar Formaldehyde in Dust Clouds", Astrophys. J., 183, 449.

[41] Dieter, N.H. 1972. "Anomalous Hyperfine Lines in Formaldehyde in a Dust Cloud" Astrophys. J., 178, L133.

[42] Heiles, C.; Turner, B.E. 1973. "Absence of H2CO 6-Centimeter Hyperfine Anomalies in a Dust Cloud" Astrophys. J., 182, L121.

[43] Dieter, N.H.; Welch, W.J.; Romney, J.D. 1976. "A Very Small Interstellar Neutral Hydrogen Cloud Observed with VLBI Techniques" Astrophys. J., 206, L113.

[44] Diamond, P.J.; Goss, W.M.; Romney, J.D.; Booth, R.S.; Kalberla, P.M.W.; Mebold, U. 1989. "The structure of the interstellar medium at the 25 AU scale" Astrophys. J., 347, 302. Davis, R.J.; Diamond, P.J.; Goss, W.M. 1996. "MER-LIN and EVN observations of Small-Scale Structure in the Interstellar HI" Mon. Not. Roy. Astron. Soc., 283, 1105.

[45] Faison, M.D. .; Goss, W. M.; Diamond, P. J.; Taylor, G. B. 1998. "VLBA Imaging of Small-Scale Structure in Galactic H I" Astron. J. 116, 2916 [small clouds in the direction of 3C138]. Faison, M. and Goss, W.M. 2001. "The Structure of the Cold Neutral Interstellar Medium on 10-100 AU Scales" Astron. J., 121, 2706 [on 3C147, the same cloud described by Dieter in 1976]. Brogan, C.L.; Zauderer, B.A.; Lazio, T.J.; Goss, W.M.; DePree, C.G.; Faison, M.D. 2005. "Spatial and Temporal Variations in Small-Scale Galactic H I Structure toward 3C 138" Astron. J., 130, 698 [observations of fine details of 3C138 objects with dramatic increase in sensitivity].

Nannielou Hepburn Dieter Conklin: Publications

Hepburn, N.; Hagen, J.P. 1952. "Solar Outbursts at 8.5mm Wavelength" Nature, 170, 244.

Hagen, J.P.; McClain, E.F.; Hepburn, N. 1954. "Radio Discrete Sources and Galactic Absorption at 21 cm Wave Length" Astron. J., 59, 323.

Hepburn, N.; Hagen, J.P.; McClain, E.F. 1954. "Detection of Discrete Radio Sources at 21 cm Wavelength" Proc. IRE, 42, 1811.

Hepburn, N. 1955. "A Photometric Study of the Solar Corona" Astron. J., 60, 163.

Hepburn, N. 1955. "A Photometric Study of the Solar Corona" Astrophys. J., 122, 445.

Dieter, N.H. 1957. "Observations of Neutral Hydrogen in M 33" Publ. Astron. Soc. Pacific, 69, 356.

Sterne, T.E.; Dieter, N. 1957. "The Constancy of the Solar "Constant"" Astron. J., 62, 147.

Dieter, N.H. 1958. "Neutral Hydrogen in M33" Astron. J., 63, 49.

Dieter, N.H. 1958. "Neutral Hydrogen in M33" PhD Thesis, Harvard University.

Heeschen, D.S.; Dieter, N.H. 1958. "Extragalactic 21-cm Line Studies" Proc. IRE, 46, 234.

Sterne, T.E.; Dieter, N. 1958. "The Constancy of the Solar Constant" Smithsonian Contrib. Astrophys., 3, 9.

Dieter, N.H. 1959. "Neutral Hydrogen in OB Associations" Astron. J., 64, 329.

Dieter, N.H. 1959. "Photographic Satellite Position Determination" AFCRC-TN-215, 1.

Dieter, N.H. 1960. "Neutral Hydrogen in OB Associations" Astrophys. J., 132, 49.

Dieter, N.H.; Murray, B.C. 1960. "Two New Applications of 21-Cm Absorption Measurements" Astron. J., 65, 487.

Murray, B.C.; Dieter, N. 1960. "Tangential Velocity Measurements - An Independent Approach to Geodesy" GRD Research Notes, No. 41.

Miczaika, G.R.; Dieter, N.H. 1961. "A Fast Technique for Satellite Position Determination with Large Tracking Cameras" Planet. Space Sci., 7, 76.

Dieter, N.H. 1962. "Neutral Hydrogen in IC 342" Astron. J., 67, 313.

Dieter, N.H. 1962. "Neutral Hydrogen in M 33" Astron. J., 67, 217.

Dieter, N.H. 1962. "Neutral Hydrogen in M 101" Astron. J., 67, 317.

Dieter, N.H. 1962. "Neutral Hydrogen in Nearby SC Galaxies" Astron. J., 67, 270.

Dieter, N.H. 1962. "A Search for HI in Centaurus A" Astron. J., 67, 222.

Dieter, N.H.; Epstein, E.E.; Lilley, A.E.; Roberts, M.S. 1962. "A Radio and Optical Investigation of Extragalactic Redshifts" Astron. J., 67, 270.

Dieter, N.H. 1964. "Neutral Hydrogen near the North Galactic Pole" Astron. J., 69, 137.

Dieter, N.H. 1964. "Neutral Hydrogen near the North Galactic Pole" Astron. J., 69, 288.

Dieter, N.H.; Ewen, H.I. 1964. "Radio Observations of the Interstellar OH Line at 1667 Mc/s" Nature, 201, 279.

Dieter, N.H. 1965. "Neutral Hydrogen near the Galactic Poles" Astron. J., 70, 552.

Weaver, H.; Williams, D.R.W.; Dieter, N.H.; Lum, W.T. 1965. "Observations of a Strong Unidentified Microwave Line and of Emission from the OH Molecule" Nature, 208, 29.

Dieter, N.H.; Goss, W.M. 1966. "Recent Work on the Interstellar Medium" Rev. Mod. Phys., 38, 256.

Dieter, N.H.; Weaver, H.; Williams, D.R.W. 1966. "The Interstellar Hydroxyl Radio Emission" Sky & Tel., 31, 132.

Dieter, N.H.; Weaver, H.; Williams, D.R.W. 1966. "Secular Variations in the Radio-Frequency Emission of OH" Astron. J., 71, 160.

Weaver, H.; Williams, D.R.W.; Dieter, N.H. 1966. "OH Radio-Frequency Emission near Very Bright H II Regions" Astron. J., 71, 184.

Williams, D.R.W.; Dieter, N.H.; Weaver, H. 1966. "Linear Polarization of the Emission from the OH Molecule" Astron. J., 71, 186.

Dieter, N.H. 1967. "Observations of the 158á Recombination Line" IAU Symp., 31, 233.

Dieter, N.H. 1967. "Observations of the Hydrogen Recombination Line 158á in Galactic H II Regions" Astrophys. J., 150, 435.

Dieter, N.H.; Weaver, H.F.; Williams, D.R.W. 1967. "Berkeley Results on OH Emission" IAU Symp., 31, 73.

Goss, W.M.; Dieter, N.H. 1967. "Model Calculations of H II Region Temperatures" Publ. Astron. Soc. Pacific, 79, 575.

Weaver, H.; Dieter, N.H.; Williams, D.R.W. 1968. "Observations of OH Emission in W3, NGC 6334, W49, W51, W75, and ORI a" Astrophys. J. Suppl., 16, 219.

Dieter, N.H. 1969 "High-Velocity Interstellar Gas" Publ. Astron. Soc. Pacific, 81, 186.

Dieter, N.H. 1971. "Berkeley Survey of High-Velocity Interstellar Neutral Hydrogen" Astron. Astrophys., 12, 59.

Dieter, N.H. 1971. "Interstellar Molecules" Dark Nebulae, Globules, and Protostars (B.T. Lynds, ed., U. AZ Press), 77.

Spinrad, H.; Sargent, W.L.W.; Oke, J.B.; Neugebauer, G.; Landau, R.; King, I.R.; Gunn, J.E.; Garmire, G.; Dieter, N.H. 1971. "Maffei 1: a New Massive Member of the Local Group?" Astrophys. J., 163, L25.

Dieter, N.H. 1972. "Anomalous Hyperfine Lines in Formaldehyde in a Dust Cloud" Astrophys. J., 178, L133.

Dieter, N.H. 1972. "Berkeley Survey of High-Velocity Interstellar Neutral Hydrogen. I. The Section $b = -15°$ to $+15°$, $l = 10°$ to $250°$" Astron. Astrophys. Suppl., 5, 21.

Dieter, N.H. 1972. "Berkeley Survey of High-Velocity Interstellar Neutral Hydrogen. II. The Section $| b | ? 15°$" Astron. Astrophys. Suppl., 5, 313.

Dieter, N.H. 1973. "A Survey of Interstellar Formaldehyde in Dust Clouds" Astrophys. J., 183, 449.

Dieter, N.H. 1975. "Interstellar Formaldehyde near Stars of the Orion Population" Astrophys. J., 199, 289.

Dieter, N.H.; Welch, W.J.; Romney, J.D. 1976. "A Very Small Interstellar Neutral Hydrogen Cloud Observed with VLBI Techniques" Astrophys. J., 206, L113.

Dieter, N.H.; Welch, W.J.; Wright, M.C.H. 1979. "H2O Masers and H II Regions in W49 at 23 GHz" Astrophys. J., 230, 768.

Selected Bibliography: Women in Science
Compiled by Claire Hooker

Abir-Am, Pnina; and Outram, Dorinda, (eds). Uneasy Careers and Intimate Lives: Women in science, 1789–1979. Rutgers University Press, New Brunswick, 1987.

Benstock, Shari (ed). The Private Self: Theory and Practice of Women's Autobiographical Writings. University of North Carolina Press, Chapel Hill, 1989.

Cockburn, Cynthia. Machinery of Dominance: Women, Men and Technical Know-How. Pluto Press, London, 1985.

Couser, Thomas. Recovering Bodies: Illness, Disability, and Life Writing. University of Wisconsin Press, Madison, 1997.

Fausto-Sterling, Anne. Myths of Gender: Biological Theories about Women and Men. Basic Books, New York, 1992.

Goodwin, James. Autobiography: The Self Made Text. Twayne Gusdorf, New York, 1993.

Haynes, Roslyn. From Faust to Strangelove: Representations of the Scientist in Western Literature. Johns Hopkins University Press, Baltimore, 1994.

Hooker, Claire. Irresistible Forces: Women in Australian Science. Melbourne University Press, Melbourne, 2004.

Keller, Evelyn Fox. Reflections on Gender and Science. Yale University Press, New Haven, 1995.

Kohlstedt, Sally Gregory, (ed.). History of Women in the Sciences: Readings from Isis. University of Chicago Press, Chicago, 1999.

Kohlstedt, Sally Gregory; and Longino, Helen, (eds). Women, Gender and Science: New Directions. Osiris, 12, 1997.

Lederer, Muriel; and Bartsch, Ingrid, (eds). The Gender and Science Reader. Routledge, London and New York, 2001.

Mason, Mary; and Green, Carol (eds). Life Prints: A Memoir of Healing and Discovery. Feminist Press, New York, 2000.

Mayberry, Maralee; Subramaniam, Banu; and Weasel, Lisa, (eds). Feminist Science Studies: A New Generation. Routledge, New York and London, 2001.

Olney, James, Autobiography: Essays Theoretical and Critical, Princeton University Press, Princeton, 1980.

Rossiter, Margaret. Women Scientists in America: Struggles and Strategies to 1940. Johns Hopkins University Press, Baltimore, 1982.

Rossiter, Margaret. Women Scientists in America: Before Affirmative Action, 1940-1972. Johns Hopkins University Press, Baltimore, 1995.

Smith, Sidonie; and Watson, Julia, (eds). Inter/Faces: Women, Autobiography, Image, Performance. University of Michigan Press, Ann Arbor, 2002.

Traweek, Sharon. Beamtimes and Lifetimes: The World of High Energy Physicists. Harvard University Press, Boston, 1988.

Wertheim, Margaret. Pythagoras' Trousers: God, Physics and the Gender Wars. Random House, New York, 1995.

Selected Bibliography: Radio Astronomy and Radio Astronomy History
Compiled by Ellen Bouton

Classics in radio astronomy. Selection and commentary by Woodruff Turner Sullivan. Reidel, Dordrecht, 1982. [Selected reprints of classic radio astronomy papers.]

The Cosmic Perspective. Jeffrey Bennett, Megan Donahue, Nicholas Schneider and Mark Voit. 4th ed. Benjamin-Cummings, San Francisco, CA, 2006. [General astronomy textbook]

The Early Years of Radio Astronomy: Reflections Fifty Years After Jansky's Discovery. Edited by W.T. Sullivan III. Cambridge University Press, Cambridge, 1984. [Papers honoring the 50th anniversary of Karl G. Jansky's 1933 discovery of cosmic radio waves, selected from sessions held at 1983 meetings of the American Association for the Advancement of Science, International Union for Radio Science, and International Astronomical Union.]

An Introduction to Radio Astronomy. Bernard F. Burke and Francis Graham-Smith. 2nd ed. Cambridge University Press, Cambridge, 2002. [College level text.]

The Invisible Universe Revealed: The Story of Radio Astronomy. Gerrit Verschuur. Springer-Verlag, New York, 1986. [Intended for the non-scientist.]

Radio Astronomy. John D. Kraus; with a chapter on radio-telescope receivers by Martti E. Tiuri and Antti V. Raisanen ; with additional contributions by Thomas D. Carr ... [et al.] 2nd ed. Cygnus-Quasar Books, Powell, OH, 1986. [Fundamental text on the technical aspects of radio astronomy instrumentation.]

Serendipitous Discoveries in Radio Astronomy. Edited by K. Kellermann and B. Sheets. National Radio Astronomy Observatory, Green Bank, WV, 1983. [Proceedings of a workshop honoring the 50th anniversary of the discovery of cosmic radio waves by Karl G. Jansky on May 5, 1933; contains papers on history of and discoveries in radio astronomy.]